Chinese Mythology

CHINESE MYTHOLOGY

An Encyclopedia of Myth and Legend

Derek Walters

DIAMOND
BOOKS

This edition published 1995 by
Diamond Books
77-85 Fulham Palace Road
Hammersmith, London W6 8JB

First published by The Aquarian Press 1992

ISBN 0 261 66657 6

Printed in Great Britain

Contents

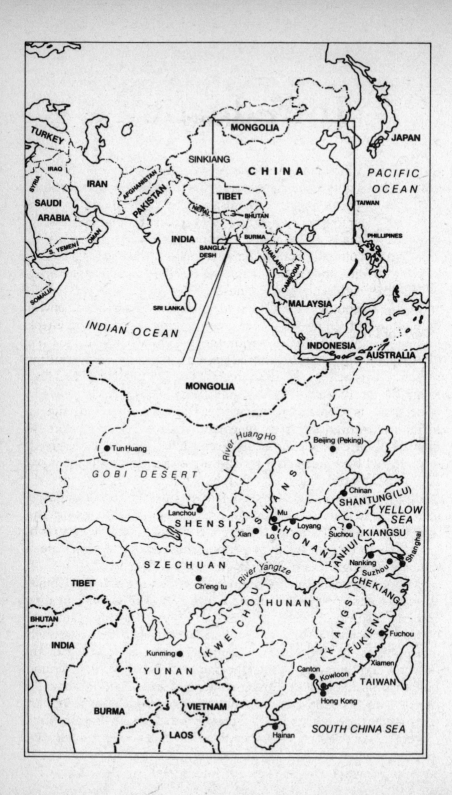

Introduction

China is vast. Stretching from the lands of the Arabian Nights, over the soaring heights of the Himalayas to the tropical shores of the South Pacific, it covers an area that in Western terms would reach from the Atlantic Ocean to the Caspian Sea, from Ireland to Iran, from Poland to Egypt. China is not so much a country as a world of nations. Yet although its culture is drawn from many lands, there is at its core an essential quality, almost indefinable yet instantly recognizable, which is what the world knows as Chinese.

For this reason, it is difficult to make a valid comparison between the cultures of China and other great empires, such as the Greek, Roman, or Egyptian. To begin with, the first unified empire, the Ch'in [Qin], from which China derives its name, did not exist until two hundred years before the Christian era, by which time Egypt had been ruled by its Pharaohs for two millennia. But what is generally understood as 'China', a nation with its unique written language, its literature, discoveries, philosophies and sciences, existed before the Pharaohs. For China had already been united, not by power-greedy despots, but by a much stronger and more enduring force, the power of the written word. The crucial feature of this astonishing script is the facility which not only enables scholars who speak different languages to correspond with each other, but even to comprehend writings that were set down thousands of years ago, enabling, for example, texts by Confucius to be read today by people whose spoken tongues are as different as English is from Arabic.

History, however, does not begin with written records, and China's science, technology and learning reach even further back in time. Generations before ancient scholars had compiled their elegant texts, Chinese masters of technology had created beautifully wrought masterpieces of bronzeware. Long-forgotten sages watched the heavens, and carefully recorded the names of the stars, not in writing, but in myths and fables. And these tales and legends tell us about the people who wove those stories, their customs, beliefs, philosophies, even what they ate and what they wore. But the imperceptible movements of the stars since then have revealed secrets of their own, disclosing when the legends first came into being.

Chinese myths and legends fall into several distinct layers. The earliest religion was shamanism, or Wu, the universal nature religion. There are few archaeological relics, but folk traditions, such as horned dancers, found all over the world and in every continent, are preserved in the shaman dancers of China, Tibet and Mongolia. This second tradition, which is really the foundation of Chinese mythology, falls into two separate categories: the supposedly historical, and the world of the afterlife. The former is recorded in the Annals and Books of History compiled in the second century BC, based on traditions and written records which were available at the time. They begin with a Golden Age, before agriculture or husbandry existed, and count Fu Hsi as the first ruler (not, it must be stressed, the first man), who taught the elements of social engineering and civilization. The remaining, more mystical, aspect of early Chinese mythology is expounded in the Banner of Souls picture, painted in 202 BC, and found more than two thousand years later in the celebrated excavations of Ma Wang Tui. The symbolic illustrations clarify much that was perplexing in China's oldest poetry, which touch tantalizingly on the fundamentals of Chinese religious belief at the time. The location for these legends is a Heavenly paradise, situated on Mount Kun Lun in the west, or the Isles of P'eng-lai in the east. One central figure is the Queen Mother of the West, Hsi Wang Mu. The legends also feature the Ten Suns, in one of which lives a three-legged crow. We find, too, a three-legged toad, who lives on the Moon. The origin of these figures is extremely obscure, though some explanations are possible.

Later, Mount K'un Lun and the P'eng-lai Isles become inhabited with many other beings who may not have been conceived when the Banner of Souls was painted. The detailed nature of the picture suggests that at the time it was comprehensive, and that therefore the beings absent from it were not known to the artist, and came into being at a later date.

The next great wave of literary creativity came with the advent of Buddhism in the early centuries of the present era, but before that a new myth seems to have slipped in: the story of P'an Ku. Most literary scholars are of the opinion that this creation myth is an importation from Indo-China. Nevertheless it is now ineradicably grafted onto the great body of Chinese mythology, and most Chinese would be very surprised to learn that the story of P'an Ku was not originally Chinese.

Fact or Fiction?

Buddhism brought to China many tales either taken and adapted from Indian mythology, or additional tales of miracles and good works resulting from the spread of the new religion. To combat the alien invasion, Taoists unravelled a new skein of celestial biography, and a fourth layer of literature grew, legends which mixed and brewed together fact and fantasy, paying no heed to the constraints of time or place. The Queen Mother of the West now rules over a nation of Buddhists, Taoists and stray folk from history who walked the earth before the tenets of the great religions were ever spoken.

It is not always easy to separate myth from legend, or legend from historical fact. Just as King Arthur and Robin Hood may have existed, so there are many names encountered in Chinese myths and legends who are at one time the subjects of miraculous fables, and at other times historical people whose dates are precisely known. None the less, remarkable archaeological discoveries of the past few years have had tremendously exciting implications for historians and literary researchers. The manuscripts from Ma Wang Tui and similar ancient sites are in the exact form in which they would have been read by the Grand Historian, Ssu-ma Ch'ien, the first person to attempt a complete history of China. Even more astonishingly, the Grand Historian's sketchy outlines of earlier dynasties have often been confirmed by the discovery of ancient bronzes, with dedicatory inscriptions which have corroborated actual details in the Records. For example, a bronze bowl excavated at Ling-k'ou, Sha-an-hsi, in 1976 gives the very date, to the day, of one of the key episodes in Chinese mythology: the Battle of Mu, when Wu Wang crossed the Yellow River with his army to launch his assault on Chou Wang, the last emperor of the Shang dynasty.

An All-Embracing Religion

An outstanding feature of the Chinese attitude to religious belief today, is that like the Ancient Greeks, the Chinese are able to accept and amalgamate any number of faiths and religions without any sense of incongruity. Such a tolerant attitude was not always the case. Though many emperors were great patrons of Buddhism, there have been others who persecuted Buddhists in the pursuit of the Taoist Way, especially when the high moral tone of Buddhist critics proved to be too censorious. Then the Taoists, in order to find favour, and increase their influence in high circles, would justify themselves by adapting current popular Buddhist tales in such a way that they lent greater weight to the authority of the Tao. On the other hand, as Buddhism flourished, many characters from China's old beliefs, such as the Queen Mother of the West, were described as living in Buddhist paradises. Taoists and Buddhists both amalgamated the oral and written literature into one; Confucius, Buddha and Fu Hsi all lived harmoniously in the Western Paradise.

The position today, in Taiwan, Hong Kong, Malaysia, or wherever the Chinese religious traditions are maintained, is that a temple might be dedicated exclusively to the worship of Confucius, or the Buddha, or some figure from the Taoist paradise or inferno, but more likely, it will be dedicated to a whole pantheon of immortals, demons and deities. True, a Buddhist monk, taking time from his austere, clinically clean halls to stroll past a gaudy, incense-fogged Taoist temple, might smile wryly at the throng of images which crowd the walls, while the Taoist priest, on a similar visit, might shake his head at the celibate, vegetarian, abstinent life-style of his neighbour. But these are specialist cases, such as teaching or monastic establishments devoted to the pursuit of one particular religious cult. Local temples, supported by the community, will honour all beliefs.

Indeed, when the first Christian missionaries came to China, one of their first difficulties was in trying to find a term which would convey the notion of a single omnipotent God. There was no word that would convey this novel idea. The closest approach, Shang Ti, Lord on High, was already the name of the Emperor of the Gods, but even Shang Ti did not preclude the existence of lesser gods. There was, nevertheless, a deep-rooted concept that everything on earth was subject to Heaven's will, in that there is abundance when Heaven's precepts are followed, natural disasters when they are ignored. From this it can be inferred that there is not so much a supreme being as a supreme power.

According to the Taoist view, this power is administered very much like that of the State, with ministers in charge of various functions, such as the weather, crops, or even disease. As in earthbound ministeries, these celestial government officials were in charge of bureaucratic departments each of which in its turn had lesser functionaries, each of whom had a name, and a celestial address, a star or constellation, for the administrative offices. Some of the functionaries were wholly supernatural, some were the apotheosis of once-human beings, perhaps ancient emperors, heroes, or renowned characters of history or even fiction, who because of their works on earth, not always laudable, were immortalized and found employment in the celestial mansions. Thus was the dreadful tyrant Chou Wang translated to the skies. Thus was the constellation Wen Ch'ang made incarnate. Thus were two Chinese algebraic symbols, Tzu and Wei, transformed by homophony into Tzu Wei, God of the Purple Crepe Myrtle and tutelary deity of Chinese Fate Calculation.

Although Taoism tends to personalize all that is animate, inanimate, and abstract, by giving everything tangible and intangible, from ear-lobes to algebraic symbols, its own special deity, the earliest Chinese philosophy, on which Taoism was founded, reduces the universe to a series of formulae. In the West's great religions, the creation is personalized: God created Heaven and Earth. In Chinese terms, in the beginning was the Great Monad, from the Monad came Duality, and from Duality emerged the Ten Thousand Things.

A Populous Pantheon

Side by side with this highly abstract view of the universe, however, we find the myths and legends drawn from folklore and religious literature. The Chinese world of the supernatural is inhabited by a strange assembly of fantastic beings. There are the spirits and fairies of primordial cultures, ghosts and demons of shamanism, immortalized heroes of Buddhist tales, celestial bureaucrats of Taoism, humans translated to the realms of gods, and a vast number of spirits and entities which cannot be computed, let alone categorized. For everything that has a name must have its own attendant spirit. The breathing of a syllable, though it be meaningless, creates the genie that inhabits it. Perhaps the most outstanding example is the T'ai Sui, the God of Astrology, whose statue is frequently found in Taoist temples, close to a shrine holding sixty individual statuettes, perhaps very crudely carved, depicting his sixty attendants. The celestial habitation of this revered and august being is not a star, planet, nor any other cosmic or terrestrial phenomenon, but a mathematical concept: the spot in space where the planet Jupiter would be if it travelled in the opposite direction to the one in which it actually does.

Just as it is difficult to transfer Western notions of Heaven and God into Chinese terms, so it is equally difficult to find accurate parallels for the numbers of non-mortal beings who have been loosely translated as gods, demons, immortals and so on. The Chinese word *kuei* is usually translated as demon or devil, as in the expression 'foreign devil' to mean a European. Certainly the ferocious statues of *kuei* which are displayed in many temples are demon-like. But the ancient use of the word indicated nothing more fearsome than a departed spirit. The nebula Praesepe, for example, was called *kuei* by ancient astronomers, because its evanescent light was thought to look like a ghost on its way to the next world.

As for the use of the word 'god', the term seems to be applied loosely to any mythological being, from nature spirit to holy man. In the same way that in the West, devout persons, real or otherwise, have been posthumously canonized to become the patron saints of all kinds of pursuits, occupations and afflictions, Chinese trades and professions have their particular legendary patrons. Lu Pan, for example, is the 'god' of carpenters, but despite the many legends woven round his name, he was more properly a historic person than say, Saint Christopher or Saint George. Christian, Islamic, Hindu and Buddhist (but not, oddly, Jewish) writers use the term 'saint' to mean a holy person with miraculous powers, but there seems to be some general aversion to the word in parallel Chinese instances.

The Continuous Process of Myth Creation

It might be thought that the more fanciful a legend, the older it would be. Surprisingly, the reverse is more often the case. The classic sources, such as the great historical annals, usually give the barest biographical details, and wondrous events are usually relegated to an appendix in the histories. It is Time and the retelling which add more detail, spice the tale with a few more astonishing anecdotes and generally weave a mystery round an otherwise credible account.

Many of China's myths and legends were gathered together in collections of a known date, which reveals that the tales related there must be at least as old as the collection. Thus, for example, when Ssu-ma Ch'ien, writing in the second century BC, mentions someone by name, it is obvious that the person could not have been born and active several centuries later.

Additionally, there are a number of positive clues which can fix the earliest date, before which the legend could not have existed. Such is the case with the Eight Immortals, characters who are frequently the principal protagonists in Chinese tales. Only one of the eight (Chung-li), as a historical personage, is older than the seventh century, while the assembly of the Eight Immortals as a group did not occur until the Mongol dynasty, or in other words, after Kubla Khan. To put this into historical context, any tale which includes the Eight Immortals, unless their adventures were grafted onto an older tale, could not have existed before, say, Marco Polo's expedition to the East.

Similarly, the Emperor of Heaven, Yü Huang, did not exist in literature before his Visitation to the Emperor Chen Tsung (998–1023). Obviously, the period of antiquity in which a legend is set is no guide to the date of its conception. So if we learn that Huai Nan Tzu (of the second century BC) is denied immortality by the Jade Emperor (manifested in the tenth century AD) but accepted on the intercession of the Eight Immortals (assembled no earlier than the thirteenth century) we can safely assume that this particular legend, again to put it into historical context, did not exist before the invention of printing.

The host of people who inhabit the worlds of Chinese myth and legend is enormous, yet while most readers of this guide would have no difficulty in reciting a dozen or so Roman, Greek or Celtic names from history or legend, it is unlikely that so many names from Chinese mythology would readily spring to mind. For that reason, perhaps more anecdotal material has been included than might otherwise be the case. This inevitably means that to make this guide manageable, no more than a representative selection of historical and fictional personalities has been included. The selective process is always a matter of personal choice, but priority has been given to those elements of legend which are known to be the oldest, and the least influenced by outside sources. While there is no denying that Buddhism has been a driving force in shaping Chinese culture, much of the literature of legend in the past thousand years has been influenced by Hindu mythology. Less emphasis has been placed on imported legend, so that more attention could be given to indigenous Chinese folklore and tradition. The Eighteen Lohan, though they are all from the Indian subcontinent, are a notable exception, since they are encountered everywhere in various forms of art.

Three main strata of original Chinese legend and mythology can be considered: personalities in the stars, such as the Weaving Maiden and the Ox-boy, or the archer Hou I and the three-legged toad; these lead into the Paradise legends, and the quest for Immortality, the legend of Hsi Wang Mu, Mount K'un Lun, and the Isles of P'eng-lai; and thirdly, there is the great battle between the tyrant Chou Wang, last of the Shang rulers, and Wu Wang, founder of the Chou. After that, Chinese written literature, historical and fictional, flourished, and often the two overlapped. A notable example is the case of Hsüan Tsang's journey to the West, which prompted two great works of Chinese literature, one a serious account of a remarkable journey, the other a memorable piece of romantic adventure. To these must be added the hundreds if not thousands of tales connected with local worthies and historic personalities who have been elevated either by imperial decree or popular acclaim to the ranks of the immortals.

The utter complexity of the Chinese language, and the paucity of material in translation means that the door to the great world of Chinese literature can never be more than partly ajar. But it is hoped that this guide will give at least a glimpse into the mysterious worlds that lie at the frontier of the Chinese imagination.

Nomenclature

Most personalities from Chinese history and literature have more than one name, and characters from Chinese mythology are no different from their human counterparts in this respect. The official name consists of the family name (the surname) followed by the given name. In addition, since the time of Wang Tan, whose family were called San Huai, a number of old-established families are often grouped together under a clan name.

The official name, however, is not always in general use. Historical personalities often have a literary name, thus Huang Ch'u-p'ing is invariably styled Huang Ta Hsien (Huang the Great Immortal). In addition, people often adopt pseudonyms or pen-names of their own choice. In this guide, entries are listed by the most familiar name, though other common names are cross-referred.

Emperors are known by their reign-name, rather than their personal name. Thus the great Emperor Hung Li who came to the throne in 1736 and reigned for sixty years, is virtually never known by that name, but by the name of his reign, the Ch'ien Lung. The one exception is the last emperor, Pu I, whose short-lived reign goes by the name of Hsüan T'ung. Many notable personalities are also likely to have a title, from Emperor to scholar. This follows the usual name. Examples of titles often encountered in literature are Ti (Emperor), Wang (King), Kung (Duke), Shih (Scholar), Chün (Nobleman), Tzu (Philosopher or prince, a more general term), Fu (the Buddhist, to distinguish from some other person with a similar name). Thus: Wen Wang is King Wen. To distinguish the title of emperor further, however, the title Ti usually expanded to the more emphatic Huang Ti, Noble Emperor.

Spelling and Alphabetization

The spelling of Chinese names and words has always presented a problem. Many sounds in the Chinese language are not heard in Western languages, and attempts by foreigners to reproduce the sounds of Chinese have not always been consistent. The Chinese government has now adopted a standard method of transliteration called 'Pinyin' but this is not yet generally familiar. Most English-speaking enthusiasts of Chinese culture are likely to have encountered an older system of transliteration known as the Wade-Giles. Though in wide use, its failing lay in the convention of showing aspirated consonants (like the Spanish pronunciation of the letter B) by an apostrophe, so that, for example, Ping and P'ing represented two quite different sounds. In the Pinyin system, aspirated letters are shown without the apostrophe, and unaspirated ones by a different letter, so that Ping and P'ing become Bing and Ping respectively. Although most people are now used to seeing Peking written as Beijing, less familiar names could be a puzzle. But as the Wade-Giles system is still in general use, and the one most likely to be recognizable from literature, the old system has been retained in this guide. Occasionally, entries which might be encountered in the Pinyin form have been cross-referred. In such cases, the Pinyin form is shown in square brackets, thus [Xian] Hsi-an. There are many dialects in Chinese, and a local variant may be the most familiar form of the names of some Chinese places or celebrities. Hong Kong, for example, is written Xiang Gang in Pinyin, and Hsiang Kang in Wade-Giles.

To help the general reader, the alphabetization of entries in this guide disregards the apostrophe where used; thus Ch'a precedes Chia, Ts'i precedes Tui. This system, though it might appear to be logical, would not normally be found in specialist Chinese studies since it ignores the fact that different sounds are being represented. Please note, too, that alphabetization is letter by letter, not word by word. Thus, for example, Chang T'ien-shih comes before Chan-shih.

A

Animals

Almanac The Chinese calendar (q.v.) is so complex that the almanac, which shows the correspondence between the various Chinese calendars, the Western calendar, and the various festivals, is a virtual necessity in every household. In addition to daily information, it is also a kind of household encyclopaedia, a compendium of hints, extracts from the classics, telegraphic codes, everyday remedies, charms and amulets, and a host of other information, but oddly, very little astronomical information that was not directly connected with the calendar.

The variable part of the almanac, changed each year, is usually printed in red ink, and the invariable part printed in black, changed only when, after years of use, the printing blocks wear out.

Unlike other Chinese books, which would be eagerly copied (by hand or press) and circulated, almanacs had only a temporary value. Consequently one would not expect to find ancient copies of annual almanacs surviving in the same way that one might expect to discover manuscripts of the classics. Nevertheless, the hoard of manuscripts and printed papers found at Tun Huang early this century revealed that almanacs were prepared and distributed more than a thousand years ago, along very similar lines to those on sale today. One such calendar-almanac is the world's oldest dated printed document. Some of the calendars mark every seventh day, indicating that the seven-day week of Western calendars had reached China by then.

Amida, O-mi-t'o Also, in translations of Chinese literature, Amitabha. The Impersonal Buddha, highly revered, and placed, with Kuan Yin, (q.v.) in second rank of importance to Sakyamuni (q.v.). While Sakyamuni taught that Nirvana was possible only through meditation, the Amitabha, meaning 'boundless light' revealed that Nirvana could be obtained through faith, and so was not confined to the ascetics, but was universally available. As a result, Amida, the doctrine of 'amitabha', became widely accepted and spread from northern India, through Nepal, via Tibet and Mongolia into China, even reaching Korea and Japan. But it did not penetrate the South, nor is there any mention of Amitabha in the earliest scriptures brought to China. It seemed to have been unknown both to Fa Hsien and Hsüan Tsang, the earliest Chinese translations of the Amida doctrines coming from Central Asia. In due course, Amida became personalized, though the origin of Amida (the teacher, rather than the doctrine) remained obscure, various sources identifying him as being of terrestrial, celestial or even lunar descent.

Analects The term by which the Lun Yü, the collected sayings of Confucius are known. Although Confucius is credited with having compiled and edited the classics, his own works are known, not from his writings, but from his disciples' recollections of his discourses. All existing copies except one were destroyed in the Burning of the Books (q.v.). After the fall of the Chin dynasty a new edition was compiled by scholars from memory, but a single copy was discovered sealed in the walls of Confucius's house.

Ancestor worship Ancestor worship is China's oldest organized religion. The term may be misleading, the word 'worship' being confused with 'veneration' or 'offering respects'. Before the emergence of a unified China under the first true emperor, Shih Huang Ti, the founder of the Ch'in dynasty in 221 BC, there were in practice a number of separate states, though what is understood as historical China is the nation which lay in the grasp of the Yellow River (see *Yellow*). The states were governed by hereditary rulers, and worship at the ancestral temple was a vital function in maintaining the continuance of the hierarchy.

Today, ancestral tablets are erected in special halls at temples, or An even at home in a shrine. The tablets are considered almost sacred, and sometimes believed to contain the spirit of the ancestor, although more rationally, the respect paid to the ancestral tablet is no more an act of worship than is the laying of flowers on the grave of a dear relative.

Ancestral respect is central to Confucianism (see *Confucius, philosophy and teachings*). Remarkably, Confucius's own Ancestral Hall still exists, maintained by a direct descendant of the Sage, at Ch'ü-fou.

An Ch'i An intermediary from the Yellow Emperor (see *Yellow*), who may guide mortals to the islands of P'eng-lai (q.v.). He is mentioned in the Shih Chi (Records of the Historian).

Animals, Twelve The twelve animals of popular Chinese astrology, known as the Chinese zodiac. The factual details of their purpose is given in the entries *Calendar, Chinese* and *Zodiac*. They are: Rat, Ox, Tiger, Rabbit, Dragon, Snake, Horse, Sheep, Monkey, Rooster, Dog, Pig. (See separate entries for each animal name.) These names are of course translations from the Chinese, and many variants are possible: Buffalo or Cow for Ox, Goat for Sheep, Hare for Rabbit, and so on. What is not acceptable is the substitution of Cat for Rabbit as the fourth sign. The Rabbit or Hare has long and universal associations with the Easter season, or spring equinox, and the Chinese calendar is always organized so that the spring equinox occurs during the Rabbit month. No Chinese source ever identifies the fourth animal as a Cat. Indeed, there are at least two legends to account for the Cat's absence. The familiar story concerning the twelve animals is that the Buddha called all the animals to him, but only twelve arrived, and that the twelve years of the cycle were named after those creatures which answered the summons. The Cat was to have been among them, but the Rat, who was supposed to have given the message, failed to do so and went in his place. Another version says that the Rat gave the message, but the Cat preferred to sleep. Yet another story says that the Cat was excluded because it had caught a mouse belonging to Maya, Sakyamuni's mother.

The origin of the twelve animals is not earlier than the T'ang dynasty, about AD 600 at the earliest. It is interesting to note that magical texts of the time refer not just to the twelve animals, but to thirty-six, each of the twelve animals being accompanied by two others of a related species. Twenty-eight of these have survived as the accompanying animals for the spirits of the lunar mansions (q.v.).

One proposed theory as to the origin of the twelve animals is that they originally represented twelve ritual monthly or yearly sacrifices, in the way that the Li Chi (Book of Ritual) specifies different animals for sacrifice for each of the five (q.v.) seasons. But there is no evidence whatsoever that the sacred edicts of the Li Chi were ever superseded; and in any case, there is the question of what would be offered at the Dragon Sacrifice.

Arhat, arahat, arhan see *Lohan*.

A-shih-to see *Lohan, The Eighteen*.

Astrology, God of see *T'ai Sui*.

A-tzu-ta see *Lohan, The Eighteen*.

Autumn see *Mid-Autumn Festival*.

B

Buddha

Banner of Ma Wang Tui see *Ma Wang Tui*.

Battle of the Ten Thousand Spirits see *Mu, Battle of.*

Bikshu Four followers of the Buddha (q.v.); the 'apostles' of Buddhism. See *Lohan, The Eighteen.*

Bird, Red see *Celestial Emblems.*

Buddha [Fo] The word 'Buddha' is used in many senses. It is most usually restricted to the historical person, Gautama Sakyamuni, also called Siddharta (in Chinese transcription, Sa-p'o-hsi-to), who founded the religion (perhaps more accurately philosophy) known as Buddhism. However, some schools of thought hold that the Buddha, being eternal, existed before Sakyamuni, and continued after the Founder had attained Nirvana.

According to Theravada doctrine (see *Buddhism*), a succession of Buddhas preceded Gautama; but there is only one Bodhisattva, the Being bent on Enlightenment. The Mahayana school (see *Buddhism*), however, recognizes many Boddhisattvas.

An account of the life of Sakyamuni must rely on varying versions of the scriptures, in turn drawn from oral traditions. The generally accepted date for the birth of Sakyamuni is 563 BC. He was born to a priest-king family near Kapilavatthu in western Nepal. His mother died shortly after his birth, and he was raised by an aunt. For the next twenty-nine years he lived in luxury, marrying, and fathering a son. But he became tired of the worldly life, left his family, and accompanied only by his charioteer and horse, set out on his quest for enlightenment. He spent six years mortifying the flesh, but found that it brought no solution. Then, after several weeks meditating under the Bo-tree, he became enlightened spontaneously. He immediately proceeded to teach (the Dharma) to a group of ascetics who had been with him during his years of self-denial, and they became the first converts to Dharma. He suffered a period of temptation by Mara (*Ma-lo*), who tried to deflect Sakyamuni from the path of Enlightenment, but Mara was defeated. For the next forty-five years he toured the northern states of India, teaching and founding monasteries. He attained the final stage of existence, parinirvana, sometime in his ninth decade.

According to some Buddhist scholars, Sakyamuni was the fourth Buddha of the present age, the next, and final, Buddha being the Maitreya, or Mi-lo Fo (q.v.).

If there are parallels between the life of the Buddha, and that of the Christ (the temptation in the wilderness, the coming of the Maitreya), then even more remarkable are the parallels between the Book of Revelation and the Perfection of Wisdom, both of which refer to the 'ever-weeping' because there is no one able to open the book of seven seals, and the need for the sacrifice of self before there could be redemption.

Buddha is nearly always transcribed into Chinese as Fo, though there are numerous variants. Sakyamuni is rendered into Chinese as Shih-chia-mou-ni. Gautama, the priestly name of the Sakya family, is rendered as Kao-ta-mo, but is not in such general use. (See also *Amida*.)

Buddhism Buddhist doctrine is a vast and complex subject, and to attempt to define its principles would be well beyond the confines of this guide. Furthermore, though Buddhism is one of the three great religions of China, flourishing throughout eastern Asia, and indeed wherever the Chinese have settled, it is not indigenous to China, and much of its philosophy derives from Indian and other foreign cultures. Yet paradoxically, though Buddhism originated in India, it no longer has any significant cultural influence there, save in the extreme north and Sri Lanka in the south.

However, the Buddhist world originally extended throughout the whole of Asia, south to the Equator and beyond, north to the Arctic, and westwards to Kashmir and Pakistan. Indeed, as the twelve animals (q.v.) of the Chinese zodiac are known to Kurdish shepherds, this may be evidence that Buddhism was carried as far west as Anatolian Turkey. In later centuries the force of Islam drove Buddhism from the greater part of the Indian subcontinent, as well as the now predominantly Islamic states in Indonesia and Malaysia. Thus, the most astounding of all Buddhist monuments (at Borubudur) is now in what is essentially an Islamic country. In China, too, there have been several occasions when the survival of Buddhism seemed to be in doubt, because of the ruling emperor's favouring the indigenous religions of Taoism (q.v.) and Confucianism. For several dynasties, however, the three religions of China have co-existed virtually inseparably.

The Revolution in China has not eliminated Buddhism, and the religion is now experiencing a revival both there and in Mongolia, while beyond the Chinese frontiers, Japan, Korea, Sri Lanka and Thailand have had an uninterrupted Buddhist tradition. Since the invasion of Tibet, the Dalai Lama, the spiritual head of Tibetan Buddhists, has resided in exile in Dharamsala, northern India. Nepal, the world's only Hindu kingdom, has a sizeable Buddhist population, with relations between the Hindu and Buddhist religious communities being extremely cordial.

There are two principal schools of Buddhism. The northern cultures of Tibet, Nepal, Mongolia and elsewhere follow the later phase of Buddhist thought known as the Mahayana or Great Vehicle, in which the Teachings of the Buddha are likened to a great raft (the Vehicle) which can carry everyone across the world of suffering to the Nirvana beyond. The term Mahayana was adopted as the universal salvation is available to all.

As other sects followed teachings which were more limited in their approach to Nirvana, they were regarded as adherents of the Hinayana, or Lesser Vehicle. Seventeen of the Hinayana sects were wiped out in the thirteenth and fourteenth centuries by the militant followers of Islam, but one sect, the Theravadan, remains the official religion of Sri Lanka and Thailand, and is the dominant religious force in Indochina.

Buddhism was first mentioned in China in the first century, but there was no noticeable conversion of the Chinese to Buddhism until the arrival of the first missionaries in c. 150. The doctrine was brought into China through the trade routes, along the famous Silk Road connecting China with Rome. An interesting consequence was that each stage of the development of Buddhist thought in India led to the foundation of separate monasteries specializing in the translation and study of each new concept. Thus, instead of a continuing process of evolutionary development, in China each successive stage was preserved in parallel.

By the fourth century, Buddhism had become the dominant religion of war-torn China, making its greatest impression in the barbarian north. It reached its zenith during the T'ang dynasty, in the seventh century, at the time when Hsüan Tsang (q.v.) brought back a virtual library of the scriptures from India. However, the Teaching suffered several vicissitudes in the ninth century, culminating in its prohibition in 845. Yet oddly, the ban, instead of destroying Buddhism, led to the printing of the scriptures: the world's oldest existing printed book, the Diamond Sutra (it can be seen in the British Museum Library) being one of the fruits of the decree.

Through the influence of Buddhism, Chinese mythology has absorbed much of the legend, myth and folklore of India. Nevertheless, the 'Journey to the West' (q.v.) can be justifiably regarded as the most significant result of the impact of Buddhism on Chinese literature.

Burning of the Books There have been several attempts to wipe out China's history and begin afresh, such as that made by the first T'ang emperor in AD 618, and the Cultural Revolution in this century. But the most celebrated occasion was in 213 BC, by the Ch'in emperor Shih Huang Ti. In an attempt to erase all previous records, and assert himself as the First Emperor, all books were ordered to be destroyed, with the exception of those on medicine, divination and agriculture. Those scholars who resisted the edict perished alongside their books in the flames. In the course of time, the damage was mostly repaired, and though there are gaps in China's literary history, they are no worse than losses sustained by other cultures through accident, neglect or vandalism.

C

Confucius

[Cai Shen] see *Ts'ai Shen*.

Calendar, Chinese The Chinese calendar is extremely complex,
dates being expressed in several different ways, which enables a cross-
check for accuracy to be made for any recorded event.

Oracle bones, the oldest Chinese documents, record the day
according to a system known as the ten stems in what might be called
a ten-day week (q.v.).

Months were, and still are, reckoned according to the phases of the
moon. The Chinese New Year is the second new moon after the winter
solstice. Years were originally reckoned according to the reign year of
the Emperor, something which is still done with legal documents in
England to this day. Thus, by the first system, a date could be
expressed as the specified reign year of a certain emperor, on such a
day of a particular moon, as 'in the first year of the reign of Emperor
Tsung, on the seventh day of the seventh moon'.

The day was divided into twelve hours, and these were known by
special signs called the twelve branches. As there are approximately
twelve lunar months in the year, the months were also numbered by

the branches and, subsequently, the days as well. By this means, the ten stems and the twelve branches were combined to make a sixty-day cycle. Finally, the sixty stem-and-branch combinations were transferred to the years, so that every year could be identified not only by its reign year, but also by its stem-and-branch number. The first such cycle began (theoretically) in 2679 BC, and seventy-eight cycles have now passed since that time.

Thus a certain day, and even the time as well, could also be identified by the stem-and-branch number for the day, month and year. These four factors are known as the Four Pillars.

The complexity of the system was smoothed out to some extent by the happy notion, probably introduced by Buddhist monks, of replacing the unfamiliar Chinese numerical symbols used for the twelve branches with twelve animal names, using names that best identified the hour, or season. Thus midnight was called the Rat hour, because rats and mice are most active at night; six o'clock in the morning was the Rabbit hour, because that is when these animals are at their busiest. For more details concerning the animals, see *Animals, Twelve.*

Because the variable lunar months do not give an exact indication of the point in time, a third calendar is used by astronomers which corresponds to the Western zodiac (q.v.). Based on this, a fourth, the Farmer's Calendar, is also in popular use. These are twenty-four exact divisions of the astronomical year, which, since each is approximately fifteen days long, can be called the solar fortnights. The Farmer's Calendar is in more general use among rural communities, and being rustic and antique sounding, adds more romance to a legend than the official calendar. Some of the solar fortnights, such as Ch'ing Ming (q.v.), indicate the times of important social customs.

Two solar fortnights make one solar month, the Chinese astronomical equivalent of the zodiac months (q.v.).

In addition to the lunar, numerical, astronomical and agricultural calendars, every day also bears the name of one of twenty-eight constellations, with its ruling spirit for the day. These are described in more detail under *Mansions, Lunar.*

Carp see *Fish*.

Cat For the factual and legendary reasons for the Cat not being included in the Chinese zodiac, see *Animals, Twelve.*

Celestial Emblems The Four Directions, East, South, West and North, represent the four seasons, Spring, Summer, Autumn and

Winter. Together with the Centre, which in Chinese is synonymous with China itself, they form the five cardinal points. The Four Directions have been represented at least since the second century BC, by four celestial animals, the Dragon for the East, the Bird for the South, the Tiger for the West, and the Tortoise for the North. Each animal has its own colour: the Dragon is the Green of Spring, the Bird the red of Fire, the Tiger of Autumn the glittering white of metal (of ploughshares or swords), and the Tortoise Black, for night, or water. The four celestial animals, which have no connection with the twelve animals (q.v.) of the Chinese zodiac, are also the names of the four divisions of the sky. The Dragon's Heart, the Pleiades, and the Bird Star are the names of three of the lunar mansions (q.v.) which marked the central position of the Dragon, Tiger and Bird. As there was no identifying star at the centre of the Black Tortoise, the appropriate place (the eleventh mansion) was called Void.

However, it seems that before the adoption of the Four Celestial Emblems, there were only three: the Feng Bird, or Phoenix (q.v.), the Dragon (q.v.), and the Ch'i-lin, or unicorn (q.v.). Bronze mirrors usually portray cosmological patterns and symbolism on the back. Those of the T'ang period show all twelve, or sometimes the twenty-eight or even thirty-six animals of the Chinese zodiac (q.v.), and those of an earlier period depict the four main emblems referred to above, but the very earliest mirrors show only the three: the Ch'i-lin, the Feng-huang and the Dragon. Because of the astronomical significance, the White Tiger replaced the Ch'i-lin, and the Phoenix gave place to the Red Bird, which is of uncertain identity. Thus the tortoise was a later but not the last addition, for many mystical texts refer to the northern constellation not as the tortoise, but as the Black Warrior.

Chan A fabulous bivalve; a giant sea-clam, mentioned in the treatise of Ssu-ma Ch'ien (q.v.), and therefore a legend of very early origin. It is said to breathe out vapours which form into cloudy palaces and terraces. (See *Po-shih*.)

Ch'an (Zen) Short for *ch'an-na*; the Meditative or Contemplative school of Buddhism, usually known to Westerners by the Japanese term *Zen*. The original Chinese word meant to resign, and was adopted because its old pronunciation, *dan*, was closest to the Sanskrit word *dhyana*, or *Jaina*. The term is explained as self-reformation through contemplation or thought.

A *ch'an-shih* is a revered member of the contemplative order of Buddhists, as distinct from the *lü-shih*, the ascetic orders, and the *fa-shih*, those who follow the laws and teachings.

Ch'ang-an The capital of the Han dynasty under Kao Ti (206–194 BC), and the T'ang dynasty under Kao Tsu (AD 620–7). Under its modern name Hsi-an [Xian], it is still a city of strategic importance.

[Chang E] see *Ch'ang O.*

Chang Kuei-fang A general in the army of Chou Wang (q.v.), in command of troops at Ch'ing-lung Kuan. During the abortive siege of Hsi-ch'i, he committed suicide. He was apotheosized by Chiang Tzu'ya (q.v.) as the spirit of the star Sang-men, and was written into the tale of the Ten Thousand Spirits. (See also *Mu, Battle of*).

Chang Lang's leg see *Tsao Chün.*

Chang Hsien Bow Spirit: the bringer of children. Portrayed as an old man with a little boy at his side. He holds a bow and arrow, and shoots at the Celestial Dog Star. If the family is ruled by the Dog Star, there will be no son, or his life will be short. The legend may be of Mongol origin, as a Black Dog of Heaven is a Mongolian astrological term.

Numerous explanations are offered for the origin of the legend in China, from the logical to the fanciful. A selection is outlined here.

According to one explanation, Chang Hsien is the spirit of the constellation Chang, the twenty-seventh of the lunar mansions (q.v.). A variant is that he is the Spirit of Szechuan province; but there is another possible explanation for the Szechuan connection.

More romantic explanations are offered through the following anecdote. Lady Fei was the concubine of Meng Ch'ang, AD 935–65, Prince of Shu. She was taken from him to be the concubine of T'ai Tsu (founder of the Sung dynasty in AD 960). The lady took with her a portrait of her former lover, which she kept close to her secretly. Unfortunately, the Emperor discovered it, and was furiously jealous, but she declared it was nothing more than a portrait of Chang Hsien, a spirit worshipped by women wanting to have children. Thus, pictures of Chang Hsien are actually of Meng Ch'ang. Other accounts, however, say that pictures of Chang Hsien are actually pictures of T'ai Tsu, though it is difficult to reconcile this version with the legend.

In a third account, the Emperor Jen Tsung (1023–64) dreamt of a handsome young archer with white skin and black hair. The archer told him that he, Chang Hsien, was warding off a black dog which devoured children. When he woke, the emperor ordered pictures of Chang Hsien to be made and displayed.

A fourth version says that Chang Hsien was Chang Yüan-hsiao of Szechuan (see above) who met with an old man who had double eyes, who offered to sell him a crossbow and shot. (See *Shun*.) Chang Yüan-hsaio agreed, and the old man told him that the crossbow had the power to drive away epidemics.

Chang Hsien, as the bringer of children, may be a play on the words *Chiang kung chia tan*, which could mean either Chiang the Archer draws the bow, or Chiang the Archer increases the birth-rate.

Chang-Kuo Lao The Second of the Eight Immortals (q.v.).

Chang Lung see *Dragon; Lung Wang*.

Ch'ang O [Chang E] The Moon Lady. Her original name was Heng O, but this was changed because of a taboo on the personal name of the Emperor Mu Tsung of the T'ang dynasty. (See also *Hou I; Rabbit*.)

Chang Tao-ling AD 35–157. Also known as Chang T'ien-shih, Chang the Celestial Teacher. Born at T'ien Mu Shan, Celestial Eye Mountain, in Che-kiang. He studied the magical arts, and was the founder of magical Taoism (q.v.).

He spent his early life travelling and visiting sacred mountains, and set up a retreat on a mountain north of Honan. He remained there studying alchemy for several years, refusing all invitations to visit the capital, and eventually proceeded on his travels, spending three years in the Cave of the Immortals. During that time he perfected the formula for the Elixir of Life. Instead of taking the pill in one dose, he took just one half of the required amount, so as to prolong his life. Though he was then 60 years old, he regained his youth and former vigour.

He left Kiangsi and went to live on the Cloud Terrace in Pao-ning, from where, at the age of 123, he made his ascent to Heaven.

He propounded the theory that illness was caused by sin. Patients were told to write down their faults, and then submerge themselves in a lake, promising its water-spirits never to transgress again. His treatments were not cheap, and his exorbitant charges earned him the nickname Rice Thief. Nevertheless, he used his funds to build up a large following of attendants and followers, and set the people repairing roads, building bridges and walls, effectively becoming the head of a pocket state.

He and his descendants were posthumously awarded the title T'ien-shih in the reign of Emperor T'ai-wu (AD 424–52) although it was rescinded by Emperor T'ai Tsu (1368–99) since Heaven could have no teacher. Instead, the title Chen-jen, Perfect Man, has been used. The descendants established their headquarters on Lung Hu Shan (Dragon and Tiger Mountain), and have since been the undisputed heads of the Taoist religion, in a similar role to that of the Pope, or the Dalai Lama.

The temple complex was partly destroyed, but later rebuilt, at the time of the T'ai P'ing rebellion. The estates were confiscated by the Republican government, but the spiritual authority of the present incumbent still functions.

Chang Tao-ling is the central figure in numerous legends. One of his attributes was the power of ubiquity, dividing himself into parts so that he could while away his time on a boat whilst simultaneously entertaining visitors to his mansion.

One day, Chang Tao-ling led his followers to the highest peak of the Cloud Terrace, and pointed to a peach-tree growing from the side of a cliff face above a sheer drop. He offered to convey a magical formula to whoever would gather the peaches. Only Chao Sheng offered to attempt the task. He reached the tree safely, gathered the peaches, and threw them up to Chang Tao-ling. But unfortunately he was stuck on the ledge, and could not climb up the smooth rock's surface. The magician then stretched his arms a full thirty feet to Chao Sheng and pulled him up. Later, having eaten the fruit, Cheng Tao-ling and his disciples Wang Ch'ang and Chao Sheng returned to the abyss. Then, leaping into space, they made their ascent to the Western Paradise.

He is represented in pictures as an old, bearded man riding a tiger.

For an incident illustrating the animosity caused by the T'ien-shih's temporal power, see *Epidemics*.

Chang T'ien-shih The title formally given, officially, to the head of the Taoist religion, and now used as a courtesy. (See *Chang Tao-ling; Epidemics.*)

Ch'an-shih Term used for an adept of the meditation school of Buddhism; popularly translated as Zen master, following the Japanese transcription. (See *Chan.*)

Chao Kung-ming The Minister of Finance, according to the Taoist classification of supernatural bureaucracy. The god of wealth, Ts'ai Shen (q.v.).

Ch'eng Huang The City God, occupying a place between the Earth God, and the T'u Ti, the gods of the locality. The origin of the practice is not known, but is an expected development of Earth worship. When a magistrate is unable to decide in a case, he appeals to the Ch'eng Huang. Pictures of the Ch'eng Huang show him accompanied by the assistant judges of the dead, Ma Mien and Niu T'ou, and processions are held in his honour on the twenty-fifth day of the ninth moon.

Ch'en Kwang-jui see *Hsuan Tsang*.

Chen Tsung AD 998–1023, Emperor of the Sung dynasty. See *Wang Tan; Yü Huang*.

Ch'i Divining lots. See *Chim*.

Chia-hsi-na see *Lohan, The Eighteen*.

Chia-li-chia see *Lohan, The Eighteen*.

Chiang Ch'ung A general, originally a member of the Hsiung-nu, or Huns, in the service of the Emperor Han Wu Ti, and the Emperor's personal bodyguard. The heir apparent, Li, who through court intrigues had already been supplanted by the son of a concubine, Chao-ti (reigned 86–73 BC) quite understandably detested the general, and tried to get him executed. The cunning general accused Li of witchcraft, and during the grim purge which followed, the heir fled the state and hanged himself. However, Wu Ti eventually discovered that he had been the victim of a plot, and had Chiang-ch'ung and all his relatives put to death. (See also *Mu-jen*.)

Chiang Keh AD 499. He rescued his mother from a band of marauders and carried her on his back for several miles to safety. One of the Twenty-Four Examples of Filial Piety (q.v.).

Chiang Shih Han dynasty. He and his wife waited on his aged mother, attending to her every whim. He walked long distances to fetch her river water rather than well water, and to obtain fish. His devotion was rewarded when a spring burst through the ground near his house, providing him with two carp every day. One of the Twenty-Four Examples of Filial Piety (q.v.).

Chia-no-chia Fa-ts'o see *Lohan, The Eighteen*.

Chia-no-chia Po-li-to-she see *Lohan, The Eighteen*.

Chiang Tzu-ya 1210–1120 BC. Also known as Chiang Lü-shang, and T'ai Kung Wang, said to be descended from Huang Ti. He is one of the central figures in the historical and mythological Battle of Mu (q.v.) between the tyrant Chou Wang (q.v.) of the Shang (Yin) dynasty, and

Wu Wang (q.v.), founder of the Chou dynasty. A brave and fearless
general, he slaughtered his enemies mercilessly, but afterwards raised
them to the status of gods. Formerly in the service of Chou Wang, he
became disillusioned with the tyrant, and entered the service of Hsi
Peh (q.v.), and later became the most able minister of Wu Wang. In
gratitude, Wu Wang honoured him with a princedom in perpetuity.

His picture is pasted up in houses in order to ward off evil words
and render them harmless.

It is said that Chiang Tzu-ya was so virtuous that when fishing he
could use a straight spike instead of a hook, because the fish
voluntarily impaled themselves on it. (See also *Ts'ai Shen.*)

Chieh-po-ka see *Lohan, The Eighteen.*

Chih Kung AD 425–514. Also known as Pao-chih; surnamed Chu
(Vermilion); born in Nanking. Sometimes considered to be the third
patriarch of Chinese Buddhism. His biography is given in great detail
in the Complete Records of Spirits and Immortals (Shen Hsien
T'ung-chien).

In 424, P'i-chia-na, a disciple of Sakyamuni, wished to return to
Earth in order to help mankind. In order to avoid being born in a
woman, he transformed himself into an infant and placed himself in
a hawk's nest. An old lady, named Chu (Vermilion), hearing the child's
cries, rescued it and brought it up as her own. At 7 years of age, he
entered the Tao-lin monastery in Kuangsi, and took the religious name
Pao-chih.

In 465 he assumed the life of an itinerant, and letting his hair grow
long, he travelled barefoot, with a pilgrim's staff from which hung a
mirror, a pair of scissors and two silk tassels. He spoke several
languages and was credited with the power of ubiquity. He earned
a reputation for being able to predict future events, and was
enthusiastically sought for his advice. However, in 483, he was accused
of deceit, and thrown into prison, but despite being put in chains, he
was seen walking about the streets the next day, although the gaoler
had him under observation at the same time. After that incident, he
was transferred to a secure room at the back of the palace.

One day, he was summoned by the Emperor to his garden, and
although it was the hottest time of the year, he appeared before the
Emperor wearing three hats, one on top of the other. Shortly
afterwards, the Emperor, the heir-apparent, and a high official died,
and the significance of the three hats was understood.

In 502, the Emperor Wu Ti, founder of the Liang Dynasty, became
his disciple, and one of the most eminent patrons of Buddhism. He

declared that Chih Kung was not an ordinary mortal, and could be permitted to wander in and out of the palace as he wished.

One of the most curious episodes in the life of Chih Kung occurred shortly after the Empress Hsi had died. The Emperor had been woken by a noise, and was horrified to see a large snake coiled round one of the beams of his bedroom. The snake announced that she was the Empress, suffering terrible pains to punish her for her treatment of the Imperial concubines. Only the Emperor's future good conduct could ease her suffering. As a result, Wu Ti and Chih Kung began work on a series of pious litanies, known as the Precious Rituals of the Liang Emperor. Shortly afterwards, the Emperor sensed a heavenly perfume, and saw a vision of the Empress Hsi, now transformed into a lady of great beauty. She thanked the Emperor for his piety, and announced that she had been saved, and was about to ascend to Heaven.

In 514, Chih Kung died peacefully, cross-legged in his chair, being 90 years old. The Emperor interred the body in front of the Ting-lin monastery, and his daughter erected a seven-tiered memorial pagoda close by.

Chih Nü, the Weaving Maiden see *Ox-boy and the Weaving Maiden; Tung Yung.*

Ch'ih Sung-tzu The name of the rain-priest in the time of Shen Nung (q.v.).

Ch'i-lin see *Unicorn*.

Chim, ch'i A common method of communicating with ancestors or the spirit world. Worshippers casting chim may be seen at any time of the day in temples throughout the Chinese-speaking world and other countries of South-East Asia.

Cylindrical boxes of bamboo slips are shaken until one falls out. This is then taken to a diviner who interprets it from a number marked on it. There are several versions of the chim, the most famous being the oracle at Wong Tai Sin (q.v.), though it is very common for families to have their own chim at home, along with a mystic book of interpretations.

Ch'in-Shih Huang Ti see *Huang Ti.*

Ch'ing Ming Bright and Clear. One of the Solar Fortnights (see *Calendar*). On the day of Ch'ing Ming, Chinese women and children wear sprigs of pussy willow, to avoid being reborn as dogs in the next life. The main activity is an outdoor picnic which incorporates a visit to the cemetery to tidy up the graves, and make offerings to the dead. The festival has many aspects, such as the carrying of willow branches (for palms, perhaps) the visit to the tomb, and the general rejoicing, which draw parallels with Easter.

Chi-tu see *Lo-hou*.

Ch'iung Hsiao One of the three Lavatory Ladies, the K'eng San Ku-niang (q.v.). In the (celestial) Battle of Mu, she was pitched in combat with Lao Tzu (q.v.). She threw her golden scaly-dragon scissors in the air, which snapped menacingly at Lao Tzu, but the sage merely waved the sleeve of his jacket to render them harmless. After her sister had lost her magic lavatory (more poetically, the Golden Bushel of Troubled Origins) to the Wind-Fire machine of Li No-cha, Ch'iung Hsiao rejoined the fray with double-edged swords, but the White Crane Youth, Pai-ho T'ung-tzu (q.v.) threw his jade sceptre, and killed her. Pi Hsiao, her sister, tried to avenge her death, but was caught in a magic box. When opened, it was found to contain nothing but blood and water, probably an allegorical reference to the functions of the three guardians of the lavatory.

Chou Hsing-ssu see *Thousand Character Essay*.

Chou Hsin (i) Tyrant of the Shang dynasty. See *Chou Wang*.

Chou Hsin (ii) Magistrate of the Ming dynasty. He was greatly feared for his severity. On one occasion he was trying a case when some leaves were blown onto the table. The leaves were from a tree which did not grow close by, and he ordered that the area be searched until they found the tree, which was in a Buddhist temple some distance away. He judged that the monks were guilty of murder and ordered the tree to be chopped down. In its trunk was found the body of a woman.

Chou Wang (Chou Hsin) The last Emperor of the Shang Dynasty (1154–1121 BC) renowned for his evil tyranny, and surpassed only in cruelty by his concubine T'a Chi (q.v.), said to be the wickedest woman in history. His reputation in legend is matched, say, by that of Nero or Heliogabalus. Among his infamous extravagances was a wine lake, in which men and women cavorted naked. It was said in those days that wise men had nine openings to their hearts, the expression being equivalent to our saying of a good man that he is 'open-hearted'. Thus when a relative, Pi-kan, remonstrated with the Emperor for his wickedness, Chou, at his concubine's request, had his heart cut out and put on display, to verify (or refute) the truth of the saying.

Chou Wang's terrestrial reign ended with the Battle of Mu (q.v.), when he was succeeded by Wu Wang (q.v.), co-author of the I Ching (q.v.). The earthly battle took place at the same time as the celestial Battle of the Ten Thousand Spirits. Chou Wang was apotheosized as the God of Sodomy, with a temple at Chi Hsien in the Wei-hui Prefecture of Honan.

His son Yin Chiao (q.v.) figures in two widely differing legends, in one, fighting on his father's side, in the other, for Wu Wang. As T'ai Sui (q.v.), Yin Chiao is the God of Astrology, revered in most Taoist temples.

Chuang Tzu The Philosopher Chuang, official name Chuang Chou, also known as Chuang Sheng, living c. 330 BC, in the state of Liang.

A follower of Lao Tzu, although his later writings took a more mystical rather than practical turn. In this he differed from his contemporary Mencius. Chuang Tzu's writings, which reject Confucianism, gained popularity during the eighth century under the T'ang Taoists, supported by the Emperor Hsüan Tsung. Chuang Tzu retired in Nan Hua, in Shantung, and consequently his collected writings became known as the Nan Hua Ching.

There are numerous anecdotes concerning Chuang Tzu, both factual and fabulous. He forbade his relatives to weep at his death, and refused a funeral, asking for his body to be left exposed to the air.

He would often sleep during the day, and dream he was a butterfly. On waking, he would still feel the ache in his shoulders. Lao Tzu told him that in a former life he was a butterfly, and, having supped off the essence of flowers, should have been made immortal. However, he lost his immortality when slain by a garden watchman who caught him stealing peaches.

The Taoist legend concerning Chuang Tzu's apotheosis is flawed by its contradiction of the known facts. It does serve, however, to underline Chuang Tzu's dismissive attitude to burial customs.

Chuang Tzu encountered a young widow fanning her husband's grave. When he asked her why she did this, she replied that she had made a promise to her husband not to marry again until the earth on his grave had dried. Chuang Tzu waved his fan, and at once the ground was dry. Delighted, the young widow thanked him, much to the amusement of the sage. When Chuang Tzu told his wife of the incident, however, she was shocked at his flippancy and inconsideration for the dead.

It was not long after this that Chuang Tzu himself died, and his wife, greatly distressed, buried him with due ceremony. (It will be remembered, of course, that the historical Chuang Tzu was not, in fact, buried.)

Shortly afterwards there arrived a scholar, Wang-sun, who had come to study under Chuang Tzu. Naturally he too was grief-stricken to learn of the sage's death, and went to pay his respects to the philosopher's tomb. Having travelled so far, he thought he would take the opportunity to look over Chuang Tzu's books, and took up lodgings with Chuang Tzu's wife in the meantime.

Within a fortnight, with the aid of a matchmaker, she had proposed marriage to the student, who was nervous about the idea, and at first objected. Nevertheless, Chuang Tzu's wife put aside her mourning and prepared for the wedding.

The student asked Chuang Tzu's wife to go with him to the grave of her husband. As he stood there, his face took on the features of Chuang Tzu, and the philosopher came back to life. The wife was horrified and ashamed, and went and hanged herself.

Chuang Tzu then burnt his house to the ground, and became a wanderer. He eventually reached the Chung T'iao Mountain, where he met the Phoenix Empress, and her teacher Hsüan Nü, the Mother of Heaven. He went to a banquet at the palace of Hsi Wang Mu, and there met Shang Ti, the Lord on High. The planet Jupiter being vacant, having been deserted by its previous incumbent, Mao Meng, Shang Ti gave it to Chuang Tzu for his residence.

Chu-ch'a Pan-t'o-chia see *Lohan, The Eighteen.*

Chu Hsi 1130–1200. Confucian scholar. A prolific writer, he edited the histories, and the works of Confucius, and is regarded as the foremost authority on the Rites. He reinstituted the College at the White Deer Grotto at Ku-ling. His posthumous title is Wen Li.

Chu I Crimson Gown, the messenger of examination results, the fourth attendant on Wen Ch'ang (q.v.).

During the time of the Emperor Teh Tsung (AD 780–805), there was a certain celestial Princess T'ai Yin, who having observed that one Lu Ch'i had the makings of an immortal, decided to marry him. Through a go-between, he was taken to the Dragon King's palace, and introduced to her. He was then asked which he would prefer: living in the palace of the Dragon King, being immortal on earth, or being a mortal with a high position. Lu Ch'i said he would like to live in the Dragon King's palace. The princess was delighted at this, and sent word to the Celestial Emperor, Shang Ti. Shortly afterwards, an envoy, Chu I, arrived from the Celestial Emperor to confirm that Lu Ch'i really did want to spend his days in the Dragon King's palace. To their exasperation, Lu Ch'i did not answer. Eventually, after further prompting, Lu Ch'i said that he had decided to devote his life to study, in order to become a minister on Earth. With that, Lu Ch'i was conducted back to Earth, eventually attaining high office and being appointed a minister. This legend illustrates the role of Chu I as the official conveyor of examination results.

Another story relates that an examiner had put a certain candidate's poor paper to one side with the failed papers, but that it was mysteriously moved back to the pass papers. Suddenly a mysterious old man, clothed in a red gown, appeared, and nodded at the questionable paper. The examiner, taking the hint, let the paper stay with the passes. So it became customary for candidates who held little chance of success in an examination, to offer up a prayer, hoping that the man in the red gown would pass their paper with a nod.

Chung K'uei The protector against evil spirits, depicted dressed in green, with a half-closed eye, and only one shoe, in the act of slaying a demon with his left hand, and tearing out its eye with his right. Often considered to be the Recorder of Hell (q.v.). Also, the patron of literature. (See also *Wen Ch'ang*.)

Chung-li Chüan The first of the Eight Immortals (q.v.).

Chung Yu 543–480 BC. Also known as Tzu-Lu; a disciple of Confucius, and celebrated soldier. When he was being awarded honours, he said that as a youth he carried ice on his back for his father, and that if his father could be brought back to life, he would carry ice again in preference to any other honour. One of the Twenty-Four Examples of Filial Piety (q.v.).

Chun T'i (Maritchi) [Jun Ti] Goddess of Light. Holy day, sixteenth day of the third moon. Also known as T'ien Hou (q.v.) and Tou Mu.

As Tou Mu, mother of the Ladle (the Chinese name for the seven principal stars of the Great Bear), she took part in the Battle of the Ten Thousand Spirits (q.v.). She is the Taoist equivalent of Kuan Yin (q.v.), although the origin of the goddess is ultimately Hindu, taken into the broader fold of Tantric Buddhism, and thence to China and Japan. She is often shown with eight arms, two holding the Sun and the Moon, and sometimes with more pairs of arms, holding various Buddhist, Tantric or military emblems; they include a bow, spear, battleaxe, sword, flag, dragon's head, pagoda, lotus, wheel, chariot, sun and moon. Her chariot is drawn by seven pigs, the number of the stars of the constellation in which she resides.

At the Semding Lamasery in Tibet one of the abbesses who was believed to be the incarnation of Chun T'i had an outgrowth on her neck in the shape of a sow's ear. Hence three-faced statues of Chun T'i sometimes depict the right face (in China and Japan; in India the left one) as a sow's.

Tou Mu, according to some sources, has a husband, Tou Fu, (Father of the Ladle) and nine sons, Jen Wang, or Human Kings, called T'ien-ying, T'ien-jen, T'ien-chu, T'ien-hsin, T'ien-ch'in, T'ien-fu, T'ien-ch'ung, T'ien-jui and T'ien-p'eng, meaning, respectively, Celestial, -Bravery, -Official, -Pillar, -Heart, -Creature, -Support, -Minor, -Bud and -Sail.

She was well-versed in celestial knowledge, and could cross oceans, from the Sun to the Moon, and shone with a mysterious light. She passed her knowledge on to her sons, and went to live in the south. There, the people were so impressed by the family that they elected T'ien-ying as their king.

Yüan-shih T'ien-ts'un invited the family to Heaven, and gave Tou Mu the palace of Tou, the Pole Star, for her residence.

Chu Pa-chiai The Pig Fairy, usually rendered as Pigsy by Chinese translators, a character in the Journey to the West (q.v.) and a companion of the Monkey King (q.v.). He was formerly a celestial official in charge of the navigation of the River Han (the Milky Way). As a result of getting drunk and making unwelcome advances to the daughter of the Jade Emperor, he was banished to the earth. Unfortunately he was reincarnated in the body of a pig, and repaid his gratitude to his pig-mother by eating her and the rest of the litter. Thereafter, he inhabited a remote and wild area of Fu-ling Mountain, where he attacked and killed people with an iron rake.

However, he was converted to Buddhism by Kuan Yin (q.v.), and accompanied Hsüan Tsang (q.v.) on his travels. For his help in bringing back the Buddhist scriptures, he was admitted to the Western Paradise, and appointed Chief Altar-Washer.

Chü-pao P'en A magic bowl used by Yüan-tan, the God of Wealth. It sprouted gold ingots as fast as they were removed. (See also Ts'ai Shen.)

Chu Shou-ch'ang Sung dynasty. His parents separated when he was young, and he vowed that he would search for his mother until he found her again. This he succeeded in doing after fifty years. One of the Twenty-Four Examples of Filial Piety (q.v.).

Cinnabar see *Elixir of Life.*

Clan names see *Wang Tan.*

Confucius, K'ung Fu Tzu [Kong Fuzi] 551–479 BC. China's greatest sage. His grandfather, related to the kings of Sung in Honan, moved to the state of Lu, modern Shantung, to escape feudal wars in his native state. His father was a military official who had nine daughters, but whose only son was crippled. He took a second wife at 70, and she bore him the son he wanted: Confucius. The father died three years later, and the widow moved to Ch'ü-fou, Yen-chou, where the family's ancestral temple is still tended by a descendant.

He married at 18, had a son and a daughter, but though little is known of the son, his son, Confucius's grandson, became a famous teacher and promulgator of his grandfather's doctrines. Confucius was given a minor position, but soon achieved a reputation as a scholar and a teacher. Confucius went to Lo-yang, then the capital (modern Honan). When a civil war forced the Duke of Lu into exile, Confucius went with him. The succeeding Duke of Lu promoted Confucius to be minister of Justice, and the sage was able to institute a number of reforms. However, the court of Lu became dissolute, and Confucius left to begin a twelve-year journey visiting various states and trying to convert them to his teachings of virtuous behaviour. Eventually he returned to Lu, and began work editing the Chinese classics, his one original contribution being the Ch'un Ch'iu, the Spring and Autumn Annals, the history of the State of Lu.

His main work, however, was his teaching, and at his death he had some three thousand followers. Neither the common people nor the court fully appreciated him during his lifetime, however, although a temple to his memory was built by the Duke of Lu.

Wider interest in the works of Confucius followed the Burning of the Books (q.v.), and after the Han dynasty every Emperor paid respect to his memory.

Confucius, philosophy and teachings The term Confucianism is given to a distinctive form of philosophy, ritual and conduct which is based on the teachings of Confucius (q.v.). It has been called the national religion of China, but there are others who claim that it cannot be a religion, since there is no personal god who is the object of worship.

Confucianism is best described as a system of ethics. While ritual plays a vital role in holding the apparatus of Confucianism together, there are of course many societies to which some form of ritual or ceremony is germane (such as a civil wedding) without any element of religious principle being present. The teachings of Confucius were collected unsystematically, firstly by his disciples, then re-stated by Mencius (372–289 BC). The present form of Confucianism is due to the work of the scholar Chu Hsi (1130–1200).

From his sayings it is apparent that Confucius emphasized the need to pay respect to the spirits of ancestors, but made no provision for occult studies. Nevertheless, he did not discount the possibility of a supernatural world alongside the material one. The precepts of Confucianism are simple enough:

1. The universe is regulated by order.
2. Mankind is basically good.
3. People do wrong through lack of knowledge, and from lack of example.
4. Government must lead by good moral example.
5. Development is inward and outward. Inward development is acting in private as if under observation. Outward development is revealed by self-sufficiency and punctiliousness.

Confucius said that the essential quality was goodness, for which he used the term *jen*. Sometimes translated as sympathy or fellow-feeling, it is to do good without any motive, even the motive of doing good. Mencius said that *jen* itself encompassed three qualities:

1. *I*, integrity, that is acting without self-interest;
2. *Li*, propriety, or decent behaviour, which Confucius would also understand to include attention to the rites; and
3. *Chih*, intellect, which enables one to form sound judgements.

To these virtues later commentators added *hsin*, fidelity, or keeping one's promise. Jen, I, Li, Chih, and Hsin are known as the Five Virtues.

Corpses It is a fundamental belief that the corpse must be buried in a spot deemed to be secure and peaceful, otherwise the soul would not leave the body and be able to rest. If someone had died away from the family grave, the body had to be brought to the spot for burial. A common thread running through popular Chinese horror films is the ability of magicians to imbue corpses with motion, though not actual life as such, so that they could be commanded to make their way to their proposed place of burial. Gruesome as this may be, the magician's role in this respect was therefore beneficial, providing a service for the deceased, and for the mourners, who might not be able to pay for the corpse to be transported in the normal way. However, magicians with this power might of course abuse their position, and cause the corpse to carry out whatever object they had in mind, be it criminal, as in committing a murder, or charitable, as in getting a team of corpses to carry out some laborious task.

The remarkable feature of such stories is that when the corpses are set in motion, they do not walk stiff-legged, as the risen dead do in Western horror films, but proceed in a series of small jumps. The reason for this curious form of locomotion is that because of rigor mortis they are unable to bend their limbs sufficiently to walk. (See also *Ghost; Human spirit; Vampire.*)

Crane Spirit see *White Crane.*

Creation In Chinese mythology, the creation of the universe is usually accepted as the work of P'an Ku (q.v.). Yet this myth was relatively late in coming to China, and has tended to overshadow China's own, more ancient, legends regarding the origins of the cosmos and the world we live in. Even more pointedly, by the time the P'an Ku myth was in circulation, Chinese natural philosophers had a considerable grasp of astronomical and geographical fact. Whatever the myths and religious dogma might pronounce about Heaven being circular, and the Earth square, by the first century AD mathematicians had calculated the size of the earth on the basis that it must have been spherical. It is quite remarkable that older Chinese creation myths not only deal with the basic outlines, such as the origin of the world and its first inhabitants, but actually include episodes which account for such detail as the tilt of the earth, and other astronomical phenomena.

According to the Shan Hai Ching (q.v.), the monster Kung Kung attempted to destroy the world by impaling Pu Chou Shan, the Imperfect Mountain, on his horn, but only succeeded in dislodging the sky, which is why the Pole Star, round which the heavens revolves, is not overhead. In the Yao Tien (Edicts of the Emperor Yao) we are told how the brothers Hsi and Ho (q.v.) were sent to regulate the equinoxes and solstices.

The older myths do not seem to have been composed by one author, but are more a selection of snippets which do not always relate. Key figures are Fu Hsi and Nü Kua, who are said by some to have been man and wife, by others brother and sister, but it is more likely that they had different origins, and were collated into one myth for the sake of orderliness.

Two similar accounts relate that heaven and earth were once united, but as a result of disorder they had to be separated. Ch'ung, the Governor of the South, was ordered to attend to putting Heaven in order, and Li, Governor of Fire, was to organize Earthly matters. Perhaps the success of the P'an Ku tale was that it was a continuous and coherent narrative which was easy to follow; earlier Chinese myths demanded a sophisticated grasp of abstract scientific facts which for most people lay beyond their concern.

See also *Hun Tun*.

Crow The sun is said to be inhabited by a three-legged crow, and sacred paintings of the Han dynasty and later frequently show the sun's face with a black crow in silhouette. It has been surmised that the legend of the crow arose through an astronomer's observation of sun-spots, described as being like a crow with three legs, though the observations made by the astronomer in question, Kan Teh (fourth century BC), are cryptic to say the least. Indeed, another interpretation of his remarks would be that the notion of the three-legged crow was well-established in his day. His remarks suggest that the crow had three legs because the Sun is yang (q.v.), and that the number three is yang, whereas two would be a yin number. If this were the case, however, the Toad in the Moon (q.v.) by the same token, ought *not* to have three legs.

The Shan Hai Ching (q.v.) tells that a crow carried away the ten suns of the Fu-sang tree one by one, while Tung-fang Shuo declared that the three-legged bird came to earth regularly to find certain herbs that were needed to prolong its life. A theory has been proposed that the three-legged bird is actually a corruption of an earlier idea, that of three red-headed birds with black eyes, who waited on Hsi Wang Mu and provided her with all her wants. One of these birds is shown in the Banner of Ma Wang Tui (q.v.).

D

Dragons

Dog The eleventh of the twelve animals (q.v.) of the Chinese zodiac (q.v.). The Celestial Dog was believed to devour the moon at eclipses, and was shot by the Celestial Archer Hou I (q.v.).

Door Gods It is customary, at the Chinese New Year, to replace the pictures of the Door Gods, colourful posters which are displayed either side of the entrance door in shops and houses. These gods are of two types: official and family.

There are several variant explanations of the origin of the custom, which was current long before the time of Emperor T'ai Tsung of the following popular story.

The T'ang emperor T'ai Tsung (AD 627–50) fell sick, and was troubled by nightmares, imagining that demons were in his bedchamber. The Empress summoned a consultation of ministers and physicians, and the Emperor assured them that he saw the visions at night. Two ministers, Ch'in Shu-pao and Hu Ching-teh, volunteered to stay up and keep watch while the Emperor slept.

That night the Emperor slept peacefully at last, and thereafter began to recover. Although the ministers still kept their vigil each night, the

Emperor told them that he could now dispense with their services, provided that their portraits were posted up in their place. This seemed to work for a while, but the demons seem to have found another entrance, and a third minister, Wei Cheng, was posted at the back door.

According to the official history of the T'ang dynasty, Ch'in Shu-pao was born in Shantung, was General-in-Chief of the left flank of T'ai Tsung's army, created a Duke, and died in AD 638; Hu Ching-teh was born in Shansi, became a brave general, was created Duke, and died in AD 659; Wei was an official born in Chih-li.

The following legend regarding family door-gods is drawn from fable, rather than history. A certain peach-tree was bent over in an archway, and as peach-wood is a sacred material, evil spirits would keep passing through the arch to and fro. The emperor therefore chopped down the tree, and erected talismanic pictures to frighten away the revenants.

Pictures of door-gods are often redolent with symbolism. The motifs illustrated are a particularly Chinese form of visual pun, or rebus (q.v.), of the type sometimes encountered in Western heraldry.

Dragon One of the oldest symbolic animals, stylized forms of which are a feature of the decoration of ancient bronzes cast before the invention of writing. In complete contrast to Western mythology, however, Dragons are rarely depicted as malevolent. They may be fearsome and very powerful, and all stand in awe of the dragon-kings, but they are equally considered just, benevolent, and the bringers of wealth and good fortune. There are, of course, legends of the various immortals battling against evil dragons, but such monsters would be foreign ones. Local dragons are to be respected, feared, and petitioned as one would petition a just and honest ruler. For this reason, the dragon symbol is the sign of authority, being worn on the robes of the Imperial family and nobility.

Dragons are generally considered to be aquatic, living in lakes, rivers and the sea, the larger the expanse of water, the more powerful the dragon. Nevertheless, there are dragons which inhabit the heavens, one quarter of the sky being called the Palace of the Green Dragon, in reference to the stars which in Chinese astronomy constitute the constellation of the Dragon. Even so, the appearance of the Dragon constellation is said to herald the rainy season.

In mythology, dragons pull the chariots of various deities, such as the Sun, Hsi Wang Mu (q.v.), and others. They are of two classes, smooth dragons and scaly dragons, for which there are separate words in Chinese, but the Chinese Dragon is not usually shown with wings. The so-called winged dragon shown in Chinese paintings has appendages which might be more aptly described as fins, rather than the bat-like wings with which Western artists portray the creature.

In Chinese mythology one attribute of the dragon is its ability to find, or rather to disgorge, pearls. Consequently these are usually shown, surrounded by flames, close to, or issuing from, a dragon's mouth.

According to the Shuo Wen dictionary, written in AD 200, the dragon is the king of all scaly creatures: fish, reptiles, amphibia and the like. It can make itself invisible at will, lives in the water for half the year, and rises to the sky in the spring (when the constellation of the Dragon is at its zenith). It is reputed to be deaf, owing to the fact that the Chinese word for deaf has the same sound, *lung*, as the word for dragon, but this is not borne out in the numerous legends which relate conversations between mortals and dragons. It is also said to be a composite of nine animals: a camel's head, a deer's horns, a rabbit's eyes, a cow's ears, a snake's neck, a frog's belly, a carp's scales, a hawk's claws and a tiger's paws.

Various sub-species of dragon have been described in Chinese literature, for example the Heavenly Dragon which protects the realms of the immortals, the Spirit Dragon which produces rain, and the Hidden Treasures Dragon which guards hoards.

With the advent of Buddhism, dragon symbolism became absorbed into the new religion, and it is erroneous to suppose that just because the dragon figures in Buddhist art, it originated there.

In Peking [Beijing] there is a famous Nine Dragon Screen which has been much imitated. The brick and faience screen represents the nine species of dragon which are portrayed in their respective places on temple roofs, sword hilts and the like. Smaller such screens may be found in any large city of China which has ornamental gardens.

Concerning the Nine Dragons, mention must be made of the name of the city of Kowloon, on the Hong Kong mainland. Kowloon [Chiu Lung] means Nine Dragons, and it is said that the name was given in deference to the Emperor: there being eight hills, or dragon mountains in Kowloon, the ninth 'dragon' being the Emperor. This reason may be more fanciful than actual, the more likely origin of the name being the reference to the nine representations of dragon shown on the Peking screen.

The Dragon is the fifth sign of the so-called Chinese zodiac (q.v.). (See also *Carp; Lung Wang; Celestial Emblems.*)

Dragon Boat Festival Held on the fifth day of the fifth moon, this colourful festival is said to commemorate Ch'ü Yüan, who drowned himself as a protest against a corrupt government. The people set out in boats to find the body, but to no avail. They therefore set out once more, with special cakes, to offer to Chü's spirit.

The festival is now a day in which boat races are held throughout the Chinese-speaking world on any convenient stretch of water. The boats, about forty metres long, are not only designed for swift movement, but are highly decorated with a dragon-head prow.

Dragon King see *Lung Wang*.

E

Earth God

Earth see *Elements, the Five*.

Earth God There are two distinct matters which may be understood by 'Earth God', the Earth God specifically, and Earth gods in general. The (specific) Earth God is one of the most ancient deities of China, and equal to Heaven. The Earth supplied all wants, while Heaven supplied fortune and retribution. Sacrifices were offered to the Earth God at the Imperial altar in the capital, while in rural villages, offerings were made to mounds of earth erected for the purpose. While offerings to Heaven were burned, those to the Earth were buried.

In addition to the specific Earth God, there are also numerous local Earth gods; these are spirits of the locality, and every place which has a name has its own spirit, while there are greater spirits which have jurisdiction over a whole administrative area, such as a city, or province. Paradoxically, perhaps, it is the Earth God and the local Earth gods which are generally more revered and respected than city or provincial gods. The Earth God is an all-powerful deity whose munificence the Empire relies on, while the local god is virtually a personal spirit who knows everyone in the locality by name.

T'u Ti (both words mean Earth in a different sense) shrines to the local spirits can be found in every village, in the streets, by the sides of bridges, and in the entrance halls of large tower blocks, with incense constantly burning in front of them. They are even found accompanying grave sites, thanking the local earth spirit for allowing the intrusion of the entombment.

For a reference to the custom of placing T'u Ti shrines on the ground, see *T'ai Tsu*.

Eight Diagrams (Pa Kua) [Ba Gua] The Eight Diagrams are symbols of mystic and talismanic power. Each consists of three lines, which may be full ——— or broken ———, placed one above the other, making eight possible combinations in all. As such, they are the earliest known examples of binary notation. Placed at the sides of an octagon they form the popular Chinese talisman called the Pa Kua [Ba Gua], Eight Symbols. It is believed to be a powerful demonifuge, and is displayed in many Chinese houses much as a Christian household might display a Cross.

There are two traditional arrangements of the Eight Diagrams, or trigrams as they are bettern known. One is commonly found on Chinese mariners' compasses, the eight trigrams corresponding to the eight divisions of the compass, with this difference. In the Western-style compass, the points, north, north-east and so on are precise points: in the Chinese compass the equivalent trigram refers to the whole sector of 45°. In this 'practical' sequence of the Eight Trigrams, known as the 'Later Heaven' sequence, the trigrams Ch'ien and K'un, represented by three full and three broken lines respectively, stand at the north-west and south-west sides of the octagon.

The other most frequently found arrangement, said to be the original form of the Pa Kua and discovered by Fu Hsi (q.v.), is the form more usually found on talismans and charms. In this arrangement, the trigrams Ch'ien and K'un are placed at the south and north sides of the octagon, respectively. It should also be added, however, that the manufacturers of talismans, whether in the form of bronze medals, or magic mirrors, very commonly make errors in their construction, as is the case with one mass-produced item sold in popular Chinese shops in great number.

Each trigram has an associated symbolism, including a numerological value and a family relationship. The family relationship can be deduced from the position of the line which is different from its two companions, an unbroken line being male, and a broken one female. Thus, the full line at the centre of the trigram K'an (the other two lines being broken) symbolizes male, and being at the centre, the middle son.

Symbolism				Compass Point	Talismanic Position	Numerical Value
☰	Ch'ien	Heaven	Father	North-west	South	6
☴	Sun	Wind	Eldest daughter	South-east	South-west	4
☵	K'an	Lake	Middle son	North	West	1
☶	Ken	Mountain	Youngest son	North-east	North-west	8
				Centre	Centre	5
☷	K'un	Earth	Mother	South-west	North	2
☳	Chen	Thunder	Eldest son	East	North-east	3
☲	Li	Heat	Middle daughter	South	East	9
☱	Tui	Sea	Youngest daughter	West	South-east	7

The symbolism of the trigrams and their names are set out above.

When one trigram is placed upon another, a hexagram of six lines is formed. The sixty-four hexagrams constitute the diagrams of the I Ching (q.v.).

Eighteen Lohan see *Lohan, The Eighteen*.

Eight Horses The Eight Horses which drew the carriage of Mu Wang (q.v.) often feature in art. Mu Wang was so fond of them that instead of working them to the end of their life, or selling them off, he put them out to pasture, something which was so unheard of that the action merited a place in history. Pictures of the Eight Horses always depict one rolling on its back, in ecstasy for its liberation from harness.

Eight Immortals Pa Hsien; the Eight Immortals, sometimes translated as the Eight Fairies by English-speaking Chinese, or Eight Genii in other contexts. Not to be confused with the Eight Immortals of the Wine Cup, a band of imbibers celebrated by the Chinese poet Tu Fu (q.v.).

The Eight Immortals or Pa Hsien form one of the most popular groups of deities in the Chinese pantheon, and are a common subject for artistic representation. The eight immortals represent a cross-section of the population, from rich to poor, old man to youth, male, female, and indeterminate gender.

At least three of the figures are historical. Whether historical or legendary, however, they are factually or supposedly from different eras and could never have met together in their human form, although all the tales about them relate that they live in the Eastern Paradise on the Isles of P'eng-lai.

Why this particular group of celebrities should have been assembled collectively is not clear. The first reference to the eight immortals as

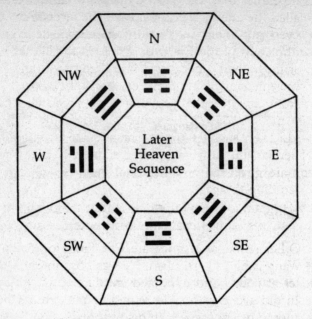

The Later Heaven Sequence

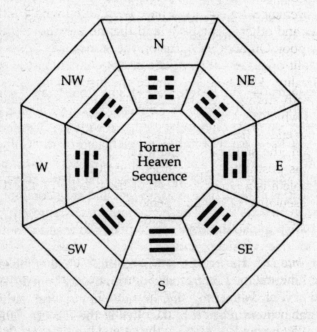

The Former Heaven Sequence

a group is no earlier than the Yüan dynasty (what in Western terms would be called the late medieval period). The legends woven round them, however, put them into wildly anachronistic contexts, for example at the court of the Emperor Wu Ti in the tale of Huai Nan Tzu (q.v.), or in the battle between Chou Wang (q.v.) and Wu Wang (q.v.). For convenience, the authentic or imaginary biographies of the eight immortals are included together. One possible arrangement occasionally met, following the order in which the eight became immortal, is Li T'ieh-kuai, Chung-li, Ch'üan, Lan Ts'ai-ho, Chang-kuo Lao, Ho Hsien-ku, Lü Tung-pin, Han Hsiang-tzu, Ts'ao Kuo-chiu.

Here they are given in the traditional order, which follows their seniority according to age.

1. *(Han) Chung-li Ch'üan.* Historical; said to have lived in the Han dynasty, Chung-li being the family name and Ch'üan his given name. Other names and titles are Chi Tao, Ho-ho Tzu (Ho Ho (q.v.)), Wang-yang Tzu, Yün Fan. He was born in Shensi, became an officer at court, and ennobled as Marshal of the Empire in 21 BC. In old age, however, he retired to Yang-chio Mountain in Shansi (not to be confused with his birthplace, Shensi), and lived as a hermit.

   There are, confusingly, other versions of his biography. Whatever his provenance, he is said to have been able to make silver from copper and other substances, and that he distributed the wealth to the poor. On another occasion the stone walls of his hermit's cave split open, revealing a jade casket containing the secrets of immortality. After he had followed the instructions, the cave was filled with strange music and clouds of many hues, and a stork arrived which took him on its back to the Isles of P'eng-lai.

   At the end of the T'ang dynasty he passed his secrets on to Lü Tung-pin, the sixth of the Eight Immortals.

   He was posthumously awarded the title True Active Principle. His emblem is a fan of feathers, or the peach of immortality. He is representative of military personnel.

   See also Lü Tung-pin (third of the Eight Immortals); *Liu-hai Hsien*.

2. *Chang-kuo Lao.* Historical; lived seventh to eighth century AD. A famous hermit of P'ing-yang, Shansi, frequently invited to the court of T'ai Tsung (AD 627–50) and Kao Tsung (AD 650–84), although he resolutely declined. Finally, urged by the Empress Wu (684–705), he made his way to the capital but dropped dead at the gate of a temple.

   Although his body decayed, and was eaten by worms, he

recovered and visited the Heng-chou mountains in P'ing-yang. In AD 723 he is reported as having entertained the Emperor Ming Huang by becoming invisible, petrifying birds by pointing at them, and drinking poison unscathed. He took the post of Chief of the Imperial Academy at Loyang in AD 735, by which time he must have been more than a hundred years old. The Emperor Hsüan Tsung made enquiries about him, but received a strange reply.

The Taoist Fa-shan told the emperor that if he dared to reveal Chang-kuo Lao's real identity, he would drop dead, and the Emperor would have to ask Chang-kuo's forgiveness in order to revive him. Intrigued, the Emperor promised to do so. Fa-shan had scarcely uttered the words that Chang-kuo was actually a white bat when he dropped down dead. The Emperor carried out his promise, and asked for forgiveness from Chang-kuo, who then brought Fa-shan back to life by sprinkling water on his face. Chang-kuo himself fell ill shortly afterwards, and returned to his mountain retreat to die, some time between 742 and 746. On being opened up, his tomb was found to be empty.

He is reputed to have travelled on a donkey which folded up like a map, and which resumed its proper shape once he had blown water onto it. He claimed to have been the reincarnation of a Grand Minister to the Emperor Yao (q.v.).

He is sometimes represented with a three-legged toad, but this may be due to confusion with another legend. (See Liu Hai Hsien, for an example.) He is portrayed seated on a white donkey, often facing its tail, carrying a peacock feather or a peach of immortality. His magical gifts are believed to bring fertility to young couples. His emblem is a paper horse. He represents the old.

3. *Lü Tung-pin (Lü Yen)*. Historical; born AD 755, in Shansi; died 805. Also called Lü Yen, and Shun-yang Tzu. His grandfather was Minister of Rites, and his father Governor of Hai Chou in Kiangsu.

He graduated in 770 at the capital, Ch'ang-an. He is the reputed author of a classic on morality, the Kung Kuo Ko, which awards merits and demerits for behaviour (singing frivolous songs: 2 demerits; studying frivolous songs: 20 demerits).

At Ch'ang-an he encountered Chung-li (the First of the Eight Immortals). The meeting with Chung-li is the core of a famous anecdote known as the 'rice wine dream'. Chung-li was in an inn, heating rice wine when Lü Tung-pin met him. Tired from his journey, Lü Tung-pin fell asleep and had an extraordinary dream in which his entire future life opened out before him. He obtained a favourable position, married and raised a family, the whole time rising in rank until he had achieved a post of some prominence. Then, after fifty years, when he should have been looking forward to a comfortable retirement, he was exiled in disgrace, and his family wiped out. At the end of his life, destitute and alone, and despairing of the futility of existence, he suddenly woke up. Chung-li was still warming the wine, which was not yet hot. Convinced of the vanity of life, Lü Tung-pin became Chung-li's disciple, and learnt the magical arts.

Some writers add that Lü Tung-pin took the disguise of an oil-seller, conferring immortality on all those that did not ask for an extra measure gratis. Out of all the customers he met, only one old lady expressed satisfaction at the measure. In return he threw rice into her well, which turned into a fountain of wine from which the old lady became rich.

He was a skilful fencer, and it is said that the Fire Dragon gave him a magic sword which could also make him invisible. He studied with Chung-li, and having passed the test of ten temptations, travelled the Empire slaying evil dragons and generally doing good.

He is portrayed carrying his sword, and occasionally a horsetail fly-whisk, symbolizing the fact that he could fly through the air. Votive pictures of him holding a male child promise that descendants will include scholars and members of the official classes.

He was awarded the title Pure Active Principle. His emblem is the sword. He represents scholars.

4. *Ts'ao Kuo-chiu.* Ts'ao Ching-hsiu, brother of Empress Ts'ao, wife of the Emperor Jen Tsung (1023–64). Released from a charge of complicity in murder, Ts'ao Kuo-chiu went into the mountains to lead the life of a recluse, clothing himself with plants. The immortals Chung-li and Lü Tung-pin met him, and convinced of his perception, taught him the secrets of perfection.

The circumstances were as follows. A graduate was travelling to the capital to take the examination, and took his young wife with him. Ching-chih, younger brother of the Empress, was struck by the beauty of the graduate's wife, and feigning hospitality, invited the couple to his quarters at the palace, where he murdered the husband. The wife refusing to comply with his wishes, he had her thrown into prison.

Later, the soul of the graduate appeared to the Imperial Censor, Pao Lao-yeh, and demanded vengeance. The Empress's older brother advised the younger brother to have the woman executed, so as to wipe out all witnesses, and on his advice, Ching-chih had her thrown down a well. However, the God of the planet Venus rescued her. While she was making her escape, she saw an imperial procession, and thinking it to be that of the Imperial Censor, Pao Lao-yeh, she made her complaint. The carriage, however, was that of the elder brother, Ching-hsiu who, on the excuse that she was being disrespectful, had her beaten with iron poles and left for dead. She recovered, nevertheless, and this time did not fail to contact the real Pao Lao-yeh. He immediately ordered the elder brother's arrest, and despite the intercession of the Emperor and Empress, had the younger brother executed. In order to release the elder brother, the Emperor declared a general amnesty. On his release, Ts'ao Kuo-chiu gave up his former life and became a hermit.

It is interesting to note that the incident of the amnesty, an historical event, is also central to an episode in the life of I Hsing (q.v.). However, the true reason for the amnesty in 637 was to secure the health of the Empress. Ts'ao's emblem is the court writing tablet and he represents the nobility.

5. *Li T'ieh-kuai; T'ieh-kuai Li.* The name means Li with the Iron Crutch; official name Li Yüan, known as Kung Mu; alternatively, Li Ning-yang.

He studied Taoism (q.v.), was taught the path to Immortality by Hsi Wang Mu (q.v.) herself. He suffered from an ulcerated right leg, but Hsi Wang Mu cured it, although as he remained lame after the wound was healed she gave him an iron crutch and sent him to teach the way of immortality to (Han) Chung-li (the first of the immortals). Another tale, however, gives different reasons for the iron crutch.

Li Ning-yang was taught the way of Taoism by the spirit of Lao Tzu directly, and on completion of his instruction, was called to Heaven by the Master. Before he left, Li Ning-yang asked his own pupil, Lang Ling, to look after his body, saying that if he failed to return to the body within seven days, he should have the body cremated. However, on the sixth day, Lang Ling received a message to say that his mother was on her death-bed, and had called for her son. Accordingly, Lang Ling cremated Li Ning-yang's body and set off to see his mother. The next day the soul of Ning-yang returned, and finding his own body gone, had to enter the soul of a beggar who had recently died of starvation. Unfortunately, the new body turned out to be misshapen, with unkempt woolly hair, and lame. Ning-yang wanted to change the body for another, but Lao Tzu advised him against it, giving him a gold band for his hair, and an iron crutch to lean on. Some relate that he then went to the house of Lang Ling, where preparations were being made for the funeral of the mother, who was supposed dead. He poured the contents of the gourd into her mouth, whereupon she awoke.

In another incident, Li T'ieh-kuai walked into a burning furnace and asked a watchman, Ts'ao Tu, to follow him. The watchman refused, and did so again when Li T'ieh-kuai stepped on a leaf to cross a river. The immortal told the watchman that the man's cares were too weighty for the leaf to support him, then stepped on the leaf himself and sailed out of sight.

Li T'ieh-kuai's emblems are an iron crutch and a gourd of life-preserving medicine, and he is usually depicted on the signboards of pharmacists. He represents the sick.

6. *Han Hsiang-tzu.* Ch'ing-fu, said to be a (great)-nephew of Han Yü (AD 768–824) (q.v.) with whom he studied in preparation for the official examinations. He soon surpassed his teacher, whom he accompanied into exile in Canton [Guang Dong], and correctly prophesied Han Yü's return to official favour.

He is said to have been a disciple of Lü Tung-pin, the third of the Eight Immortals. He was taken to the top of the Immortalizing Peach Tree, and dropped off, attaining immortality in the descent.

His Emblem is a flower-basket and he represents the cultured classes.

7. *Lan Ts'ai-ho.* The origin, indeed the sex, of Lan Ts'ai-ho is obscure, but the remark 'Though he was a man, he did not understand how to be a man,' may be a clue to his sexual orientation. Supposedly of the T'ang dynasty, Lan Ts'ai-ho roamed around in a tatty blue gown, and a black wooden belt, wearing only one shoe. In summer, Lan Ts'ai-ho wore padded underclothes, and in winter slept in the snow. Singing and keeping time with a stick, the mendicant strung cash on a cord or threw it on the ground for the poor. One day in Anhui, drinking too heavily at an inn, Lan Ts'ai-ho passed out, and was carried away on a cloud, leaving behind the shoe, blue robe, belt and castanets.

Lan Ts'ai-ho's emblem is a lute. He represents the poor.

8. *Ho Hsien-ku.* Born *c.* AD 700 in Canton [Guang Dong], daughter of Ho T'ai. Six hairs were growing on the crown of her head at birth, and she never gained any more.

She is portrayed as a young maiden, holding a magic lotus given to her by Lü Tung-pin, and sometimes playing on the sheng, a reed mouth-organ. Despite the remark concerning her six hairs, she is always shown with a full head of hair.

Not far from her birth-place was a range of hills called the Mother of Pearl Mountains, on account of the semi-precious stones found there. In a dream, she was told to powder and eat one of the stones, which she did, and attained immortality. She spent most of her time floating around the mountains, picking berries which she brought to her mother. She was foster-mother to T'ai Sui (q.v.).

The Empress Wu (AD 684–705) invited her to court, but on the way there she disappeared from view. She reappeared in AD 750 at the Temple of Ma Ku (q.v.) and again in Canton some years afterwards.

Her emblem is a lotus and she represents unmarried girls. (See also *Eight Immortals Crossing the Sea; Hsien.*)

Eight Immortals Crossing the Sea The story of the Eight Immortals crossing the sea is a favourite subject for Chinese pictorial and operatic representation. The Eight Immortals (q.v.), seeking adventure, decided to pay a visit to the world to find what wonders might be there. This meant they would have to leave the P'eng-lai Isles and journey across the sea, but instead of travelling by air, seated on clouds, they decided they would prefer a sea crossing, and to that end they employed their respective emblems for boats: Chung-li Ch'üan his feather fan; Chang-kuo Lao his paper horse; Lü Tung-pin his sword; Ts'ao Kuo-chiu his writing tablet; Li T'ieh-kuai used his iron crutch; Han Hsiang-tzu his flower basket; Lan Ts'ai-ho his lute; Ho Hsien-ku her lotus.

The octet had several hostile encounters during their journey, which they were able to survive through the magic power residing in their various emblems. (See also *Hsien.*)

Eight Immortals of the Wine Cup Not to be confused with the Eight Immortals, in imitation of whom they were so styled, the Eight Immortals of the Wine Cup are celebrated inebriate poets of the T'ang dynasty, 'immortalized' in verse by the great poet Tu Fu (q.v.). They are Ho Chih-chang (AD 659–?), Li Po (the most celebrated of all) (699–762), Su Chin, Chiao Sui, Wang Chin, Ts'ui Tsung-chih, Li Shu-chih, and Chang Hsü.

Li Po ranks first among the Chinese poets. It was said that his mother bore him after being penetrated by the T'ai Sui (q.v.), the imaginary planet which rules the calendar. Ho Chih-chang, a courtier, was so impressed by the young Li Po's versification that he declared him to be an Immortal, and Li Po soon became a favourite of the Emperor. Unfortunately this earned him many enemies and put him in danger of his life on several occasions, eventually resulting in banishment which lasted until his final decade.

Elements, The Five The theory of the Five Elements, central to Chinese philosophy since Han times, was put forward, coincidentally, at the same time that the Ancient Greeks conceived the notion of the Four Elements, Air, Earth, Fire and Water; the Chinese Five Elements are Wood, Fire, Earth, Metal and Water. The coincidence is remarkable, but it is difficult to see how one idea could have been transferred from one culture to another. No matter how unlikely, even if it could be demonstrated that the theory was transferred from one culture to another, it would remain to be explained why there should be such a radical variation in the two systems. It is doubtless a curious example of the phenomenon whereby similar ideas sprout at the same time in two widely different locations.

The essential distinguishing feature of the Chinese Five Elements is that unlike the Four, they do not balance, but remain in a constant state of flux.

The elements may be arranged in a number of sequences, but the two usually encountered are the productive sequence and the destructive. In the productive sequence, each element generates the next, so that Wood (burns and so) produces Fire, Fire (leaves ash behind, and so) produces Earth, Earth (contains the ore which) produces Metal, Metal (melts, as ice) produces Water, and Water (nourishes plant-life, and so) produces Wood.

This theory was central to the doctrine of the Five Emperors, Wu Ti (q.v.), on which the first Emperor of China, Shih Huang Ti (q.v.), staked his authority.

In the destructive sequence, each element destroys the next-but-one of the productive sequence: so Wood destroys Earth by drawing strength from it; Fire melts Metal; Earth pollutes Water; Metal chops down Wood; and Water puts out Fire.

It is important to understand the sequences when reading of the battles of various gods and demons, who often vanquished the opposing forces through the use of the appropriate element.

Each element has its own symbolism, and appropriate attributes pertaining to the directions, seasons of the year, and colours. Thus Fire is the element of heat, so it must be appropriate to the summer and the South, and as red is a fiery colour, its colour is red. Conversely, for similar reasons, Water is cold, appropriate for winter, the North, and darkness. By extension, East represents the spring, so its element is Wood, and autumn is associated with the West, and Metal, since metal implements are used to cut the harvest. The remaining element, Earth, represents the Centre, from which the other directions proceed. Its colour is Yellow (q.v.), because that was the predominant colour of the earth in the Middle Kingdom: China.

By further extension, the five elements are associated with the five planets, and of course, the spirits and deities which inhabit them.

The Earth has always been revered as a deity in its own right, but the worship of the other elements was not known until the T'ang dynasty. By then the worship of the Five Emperors, associated with the Five Directions, had been firmly established.

The numbers of spirits and guardians of the elements is legion, and the following are only a few examples of the ministers, assistant spirits, and regional variants which have been revered at one time or another in temples throughout China.

Mu Kung, the Duke of Wood, or Tung Wang Kung, Lord of the East, rules the East and the element Wood. His servants are Hsien T'ung, the Immortal Youth, and Yü Nü, the Jade Maiden. He is the recorder of the Immortals.

There are several Fire spirits, and a whole Ministry of Fire, to attend to that element, and different regions have their own fire-gods to protect or avenge them. Ch'ih Ching-tzu is one such personification of Fire, shown dressed entirely in flame colours, but with a blue cap like the blue tip of a flame. Chu Jung is another fire spirit whose human form is ascribed to the legendary period, either under Hsüan Tüan (2698–2598 BC) or Ti K'u (2436–2366 BC). Another favourite Fire Spirit is Hui Lu, a musician who also lived in the time of Ti K'u.

Shen Nung (q.v.) on attaining the throne adopted the element Fire as his emblem, and was known as Yen Ti, the Ardent Emperor, as in Chinese the character for 'ardent' consists of the character for fire repeated.

The Earth element has long been represented by the Earth God (q.v.) and various locality and city deities; while the Metal element is served by the gods of war, and Hsi Wang Mu (q.v.), who rules the West, its associated element.

One of the most important celestial ministries administers the Water Element. Floods have always been a recurrent disaster in China, and it has always been vital to maintain the favourable support of the gods in charge of Water. The Shui Fu, or Department of Water, is ruled over by the Dragon King, who in turn rules over the spirits who supervise the Four Seas.

There are also spirits of fresh water, including gods for the four main rivers, Yangtze-kiang, Huang Ho (the Yellow River), Huai and Chi, and other water-spirits and dragons in charge of the tributaries. Perhaps the one of greatest historic importance is the River Lo, for it was from that river that the tortoise emerged, bearing on its back the mystic diagrams called the Lo Shu (q.v.) which inspired the patriarch Fu Hsi (q.v.). The spirit of the River Lo is generally said to be either Mi Fei, the daughter of Fu Hsi, who drowned in the river, or Queen Chen (q.v.).

Direction Spirits, associated with the Five Elements, are not confined to China, of course. Adding to the number of direction and element spirits are the gods of Hinduism, which penetrated Tibetan Buddhism, and were adopted and adapted by Taoists. However, the foreign (non-Chinese) origin of such legends is at once evident, since they are ultimately derived from the spirits of the four cardinal points, excluding the Centre, while Chinese practice would instinctively turn to the Five Directions as a foundation. The following are the names of the Spirits who rule the Four Directions. The names are respectively the Chinese Buddhist name; the Taoist name; the Sanskrit name; and the Japanese Buddhist name. Outside China, the associated colours vary according to the cult, particularly when the Western influences and the Four Element theory have predominated.

East, Spring: Ch'ih Kuo, The Governor of the Country; Mo-li Ch'ing, Green Spirit; Dhritarashtra; Jikoku.
Colour: China, blue-green; Tibet, white, or blue for Air.

South, Summer: Tseng Chang, Increasing Magnificence; Mo-li Hung, Red Spirit; Virudhaka; Komoku.
Colour: China, red; Tibet, green, yellow for Earth.

West, Autumn: Kuang Mu, Greatly Seeing Eyes; Mo-li Hai, Spirit of the Sea; Virupaksa; Zocho.
Colour: China, white; Tibet, red for Fire.

North, Winter: To Wen, All-Listening Ears; Mo-li Shou, Spirit of Long Life; Vaisarvana (Kuvera); Bishamon.
Colour: China, black; Tibet, yellow, blue-green for Water.

Elixir of life From the second century BC, Taoist alchemists sought the elixir of life, which would grant extended life and even, possibly, immortality, and the philosopher's stone to produce enough gold to enjoy the added years. In some cases, the priorities were reversed; for with sufficient gold, it would be possible to afford the costly ingredients necessary to make the elixir.

The elixir to prolong one's years ought not to be confused with immortality, but for many people it was. Immortality was for the next world, and could be attained by good works, but there were those who sought an elixir that would give renewed youth and eternal years in this world.

Certain herbs and reagents, real and imaginary, have traditionally been regarded as having rejuvenating or immortalizing properties. The Queen Mother of the West's peaches of immortality not being freely available, other favoured potions have included ginseng (q.v.), jade (q.v.), the fungus of immortality, and deer's testicles. Powdered mother of pearl was said to have been the secret of the longevity of P'eng Tsu (q.v.). Yellow arsenic (orpiment), and mercuric sulphide (cinnabar) have been tried with dramatically sudden but unwelcome results. Cinnabar is still sold at an inflated price as a rejuvenating medicine in China.

(See additional references under *Huai Nan Tzu; Paradise; Tao; Wu Ti.*)

Epidemics Epidemics are due to the evil ministrations of the Five Devils, and there are two versions regarding their origin. In the first, the Five Persons were seen in the air, clothed in the five colours and each carrying symbolic objects: a spoon and vase, a leather bag and sword, a fan, a club, and a jug of fire. That year there were many epidemics, and the Emperor had a temple built to the Five Plague Spirits. Sacrifices were offered to them on the fifth day of the fifth moon.

A later version adds considerably more detail, and is interesting in that it introduces the Master Taoist, Chang T'ien-shih (q.v.).

In this version, the Five Devils were sent by the Jade Emperor to be incarnated on Earth, and became renowned scholars in various parts of the Empire. In AD 627, the new Emperor, Li Shih-min, sent out for all learned scholars to attend an examination in the capital. Like many scholars who failed to reach their destination, the five scholars were robbed on the way. They eventually met up in the temple of San-i Ko, but by then they had missed their chance to take their examination. As they were needy, they decided to form themselves into a band of strolling musicians. Being talented, their performances were so good that they soon attracted the attention of the Emperor, and became part of his retinue.

It so happened that the Emperor was at variance with Chang T'ien-shih the Master Taoist, who had refused to pay taxes. Listening to the musicians gave the Emperor an idea for disposing of him. He hid the musicians in a cellar under his throne room, and arranged for a signal to be given for them to play or cease as demanded. He invited the Master Taoist to a dinner, and half-way through, gave the secret signal to the musicians. The Emperor claimed that the noise was being made by devils, and told the Taoist to exterminate the pests on pain of death.

The Taoist tried using his magic mirror to quell the demons, though of course without success. However, he soon found out the ruse, and by magic or natural means, had the musicians put to death. The Emperor could not fault the Taoist, as he had carried out the Emperor's orders.

By an ironic twist of fate, the spirits of the five murdered musicians returned to haunt the Emperor, who told them that the T'ien-shih was responsible for their plight. The spirits therefore went to plague the Master Taoist until he had returned them to life. Accordingly, the Taoist agreed to give each of them a magical present with which to torment the Emperor and his court until he had raised them to the status of immortals. To one he gave a fan which gave people chills, the second a gourd of fire which produced fever, the third a metal headband which produced migraines, the fourth a stick of wolves' teeth to produce aches and pains, and the fifth a cup of water to make people break into sweats.

As a result, the Emperor apologized for his actions towards the Taoist, and re-consecrated the temple of San-i Ko in the names of the Five Plague Spirits.

F

Fabulous races — I-mu Kuo

Fabulous races Among the many legends and fables of China are what might be called travellers' tales, which gave an exaggerated, distorted or plain fabricated view of the world beyond. Stories of distant kingdoms, their peoples and customs were perhaps even more popular in the days when travelling was a privilege granted to very few. The beasts and anthropological curiosities described in early Chinese picture books differed from Western medieval bestiaries in only one respect: Chinese books were printed, and therefore more widespread. Western bestiaries are for the most part derived from the writings of Herodotus, who, belonging to a seafaring nation, had a rich source of sailors' tales to draw upon. The longer examples given below (in inverted commas) are taken verbatim from the great Imperial Encyclopaedia (q.v.), although this in turn based its content on earlier writings. As will be seen, some of the descriptions, such as that of the 'Little People' are not so wide of the mark, while the stories of people with three faces, or several arms, are reminiscent of religious statues in Hindu and Tantric Buddhist temples in India and Tibet. Their most likely sources would have been descriptions or even illustrations of them brought back by merchants travelling along the Silk Route to

India and the West. But in other cases, the source seems to be no other than the author's own imagination, and have as little basis in fact as the Man in the Moon.

I-mu Kuo: 'One-Eyed Land is beyond the North Sea. Its people have one eye in the middle of the face, but their hands and feet are ordinary.'

Hsiao-jen Kuo: 'In the east is Little-People Land. The people are called the Ching. Their height is nine inches and if a seagull finds them, it devours them. Therefore they always travel in groups.'

Nieh-erh Kuo: 'Whispering-Ear Land is to the east of No-Belly Land. The people are striped like tigers, and have long ears which reach their waists, and have to be held as they walk.'

San-shen Kuo: 'Three Body Land is to the east of Chisel-Tooth Land. Its people have one head and three bodies.'

San-shou Kuo: 'Three Head Land is to the north of Hsia-hou-sh'i. Its people have one body and three heads.'

Ting-ling Kuo: 'Ting-ling Land is situated in the Inner Sea. The people have hair growing down from their knees, and have horses' hooves. They travel swiftly, whipping their own legs, and can cover a hundred miles in a day, so it would take them two years to reach Ying-t'ien.'

Yü-min Kuo: 'To find the Feathered People Land, go to the south-east, then ask again; they are a very timid people, and do not travel about. Very tall, they hatch out of eggs, have wings in place of arms, and can fly a little.' The notion of the feathered people may be derived from stories of flying squirrels or lemurs from South-East Asia.

For examples of fabulous animals, see *Dragon; Phoenix; Unicorn.*

Fa-hsien AD 374–460. A Buddhist monk, family name Kung, born in Shansi. He travelled to India, returning to China in 414, and settled in Nanking. The stories of his travels, called the Fokuo Chi, Records of Buddhist Kingdoms, appeared in book form in 420. When he died he was transported to the Western Paradise, Hsi T'ien, and received by Hsi Wang Mu (q.v.).

Fa-na-p'o-ssu see *Lohan, The Eighteen.*

Fa-she-lo Fu-to-lo (Fa-she-na-fu-to) see *Lohan, The Eighteen.*

Fang-shih A term literally meaning 'direction scholar', referring to someone skilled in magical arts, alchemy, physiognomy, astrology, divination, and the like. The curious term stems from an original Chinese belief that knowledge of the correct orientation gave one the mastery over any set of circumstances. The term is coincidentally and confusingly similar to *feng-shui* (q.v.), this being the craft, and *fang-shih* the practitioner. Many of the official histories have appendices which give brief biographies of notable people of the times, and these often include *fang-shih*.

Fa-shih A Buddhist monk or revered person belonging to the teaching or literary orders of Buddhism, as distinct from *ch'an-shih* (q.v.) or *lü-shih* (q.v.).

Feng Huang see *Phoenix*.

Feng Lin An officer serving under Chiang Tzu-ya (q.v.) who was killed at the siege of Hsi Ch'i. He was apotheosized by Chiang Tzu-ya (q.v.) as the spirit of the star T'iao K'o, and was written into the tale of the Ten Thousand Spirits. (See *Mu, Battle of.*)

Feng-Shui Not to be confused with *fang-shih* (q.v.), *feng-shui* is the art of ensuring that everything is in harmony with its surroundings. There are two kinds: yang, which deals with the orientation of buildings, and yin, dealing with graves and tombs. Many ghost stories and legends take as their starting-point the fact that because of a bad *feng-shui*, the corpse is unhappy with its grave, and consequently returns to haunt the living.

Filial piety Regard and reverence for the parents is one of the fundamental pillars of Chinese social culture. The models of behaviour are listed in a famous tract known as the Twenty-Four Examples of Filial Piety, and further remarks will be found in this guide under that heading, while the twenty-four examples themselves are to be found under their respective headings. Here, mention might be made of one other example which has not made the list of twenty-four.

A young flower-seller was concerned for her father's health, and despaired at not being able to help him. Friends of hers were about to make a pilgrimage to Miao Feng Shan, but she could not leave her father to make the journey herself. She therefore enquired how far it was to the temple, and being told it was twenty-five thousand paces, every evening she lit incense and began to walk up and down the courtyard, counting her steps, until she was exhausted. Eventually, she reached the figure at the same time that the pilgrimage arrived at the temple. It was believed that the greatest honour and benefit would go to those who entered the temple first, and a great crowd were waiting for the temple doors to be opened at dawn. A rich official, however, bribed his way to the front of the crowd, as he had many faults which needed to be expiated. But when the doors were opened, to his consternation a stick of incense was already burning. When he related the fact to the pilgrims outside, the flower-seller's friend told him what the girl had been planning to do. Chastened by the experience, the official returned to ..nd the flower-seller, and for her filial piety provided her with the means to effect her father's recovery.

Fire see *Elements, The Five.*

Fish Ornamental fish are very popular in China and the Far East, not only for their aesthetic and soothing qualities, but also for their power to bring good fortune and harmony. The word *yü*, fish, has the same sound as the word for super-abundance. Red carp are symbolic of life, and an odd number of fish are said to avert evil omens in the home. Among other popular beliefs, the carp is a symbol of long life and perseverance. The sturgeon is believed to swim forward up the Yellow River, until the most resolute and steadfast reach the Dragon's Gate (Lung-men), beyond which they are turned into dragons. Thus the sturgeon signifies success in passing examinations.

It is well known that fish often swallow peculiar objects, such as rings and other small objects of jewellery, which are later found in their stomachs, but for the Chinese, carp are reputed to swallow letters, and have thus come to symbolize secret correspondence. (See also *Hsüan Tsang.*)

Five The dominating role of the Five Elements (q.v.) has led to the arbitrary classification of everything, living, inanimate and abstract, into divisions of five. In addition to the astrological and philosophical classifications which relate to the five elements proper (listed under that entry) the following groupings are touched on elsewhere in this guide.

Five Virtues: Piety; Uprightness; Manners; Knowledge; Trust (see *Filial piety*).

Five Blessings: Long life; Wealth; Peace; Virtue; Fame (see *Fu Lu Shou*).

Five Canons (Sacred Books): I Ching (q.v.); Shih Ching (Book of Odes); Shu Ching (Book of History); Li Chi (Book of Ritual); Ch'un Ch'iu (Spring and Autumn Annals) (see *Sacred Books of China*).

Five Beasts for Sacrifice: Ox, Sheep, Pig, Dog, Fowl (see *Animals, Twelve*).

Five Classes of Spiritual Beings:

1. Kuei hsien: Ghosts, with no bodies, denied rest or abode.

2. Jen hsien: Humans who have attained immortality in heaven.
3. Ti hsien: Humans on earth who have succeeded in ridding themselves of mortal requirements — living saints.
4. Shen hsien: Non-human spirits who have been on earth, assuming mortality, and have now returned to immortality.
5. T'ien hsien: Gods who have perpetual life in paradise.

Five Elements see *Elements, The Five.*

Five Emperors see *Wu Ti.*

Five Rams of Canton The city emblem of Canton [Guangdong] is five 'yang' which the Chinese themselves invariably translate as Five Rams. Although the statue of the Five Rams is a tourist attraction in Canton, it was only erected in 1951 as a reminder of the city's legendary foundation. According to tradition, more than two thousand years ago, five immortals clad in robes of the five colours, black, green, yellow, red and white, descended to Guangzhou on five similarly coloured rams, each of the ovine steeds bearing a grain of rice in its mouth. When the rams touched the ground, they became five stones, but the five grains of rice remained and flourished. From these, the people learnt to cultivate rice.

Like many legends of western Europe, the tale probably relates to a stone circle of even more ancient origin, and whose distant architects have perished with their long-forgotten culture.

According to the Chinese authorities, the Monastery of the Five Rams was built over the spot where the gods landed, but was demolished in 1918, the actual site now being occupied by a primary school. The original standing stones have long since vanished. However, Wuxian Tzu, a Taoist temple of the Five Immortals, still stands in the same locality, and as it has ancient sculptures of the Five Rams, it is likely that these are relics from the old monastery. The temple itself is very ancient, and was probably part of the original monastery. (See also *Sheep.*)

Fox spirits Certain spirits are said to take the form of foxes, and the animals have been worshipped in order to assure good fortune. In folklore, fox spirits often take the form of beautiful women, and wreak havoc in love affairs. They are also associated with the civil service; Chinese officials kept their seals in a 'fox-box'; an official's clerk who could not find urgent papers would light incense before the shrine of the fox spirit, after which the required document would be seen peeking out through the stacks of manuscripts.

Fu-hsi [Fu-xi] The first of the Chinese emperors of legendary times. His reign reputedly spanned the years 2953–2838 BC, other sources suggesting 2852–2738.

His mother conceived him through a celestial breath, and after carrying him for the significant period of twelve years, gave birth to him at a place called Ch'eng Chi, tentatively identified as being near Hsi-an [Xian]. According to the histories, up till his birth humanity had lived like beasts, clad in animal skins and eating raw flesh. He taught the people to hew wood, hunt, fish, cook, and make musical instruments, and instituted monogamous marriage. He is also credited with the invention of the Eight Diagrams (q.v.) and the Lo Shu (q.v.) revealed to him on the back of a mysterious tortoise. He was succeeded by Shen Nung (q.v.). (See also *Nü Kua; Yü.*)

Fu Lu (Lo) Shou The three gods of happiness, good fortune, and long life, usually seen together as a group of three ornamental figurines, though sometimes Lu Shen is absent from the trio. Fu Shen is the Spirit of Happiness, Lu Shen the Spirit of Good Luck, and Shou Shen the Spirit of Longevity. Strictly speaking, being Shen, and not Hsien (q.v.), they are supernatural beings, spirits who have never taken mortal form, unlike the Hsien, mortals who have attained immortality. Nevertheless, history or tradition is always ready to provide biographical details.

The Emperor Wu Ti (AD 502–50) liked to be entertained by dwarfs, and demanded them for his retinue to such an extent that families were being distressed. At last, Yang Ch'eng, an adviser to his court pointed out that while the dwarfs were his subjects, they were not his slaves. The Emperor heeded his remarks, and allowed the dwarfs the freedom to return to their families. As a result, statues of Yang Ch'eng were set up in gratitude for his intercession. He is usually shown in blue official robes.

Lu Shen was originally Shih Fen, a scholar, who became an official under Emperor Ching Ti (156–140 BC). He became extremely rich, and a by-word for honours and high office.

Shou-hsing Lao T'ou-tzu (Shou Lao) is the third member of the trio, portrayed surrounded by the symbols of longevity, riding a deer, perhaps with the fungus of life at his feet, or carrying a staff of the plant, but he is more likely to be carrying a huge peach of immortality. He can be identified by his large forehead, and is usually dressed in yellow.

Fu-sang Tree A tree on which the Ten Suns (q.v.) resided, with a wingless dragon curled round its base. It was located somewhere in the east, in the Valley of the Morning, because the sun rose from it, but its more precise location is not clear: while it was situated in paradise, it certainly could not be on Mount K'un Lun (q.v.), as that was the Western Paradise, yet there are no references to its growing on the P'eng-lai Isles (q.v.). (See also *Crow.*)

G

God of Literature

Gao-yao see *Kao-yao*.

Ghosts The word for ghost in Chinese is *kuei*, a word which also becomes translated as demon, imp and devil, which do not convey the sense of the word, unless, in the context, the entity is particularly malevolent. To glean some idea of the original concept of kuei, it is worth noting that a nebula, Praesepe, is called 'the Carriage of Kuei', and that an earlier description of the nebula likened it to a cloud of pollen blown from a willow-tree. Consequently, a kuei must have the wraithlike appearance of a cloud of pollen, which description better fits our notion of a ghost, than that of a demon, devil or imp. Nevertheless, with the advent of Buddhism, the idea of Hell was introduced to China, together with stories of terrible supernatural creatures who rule over the dead, and in this context the terms demon and devil obviously convey the sense far more accurately. But whether kuei are ghosts or demons is immaterial; though they may now be supernatural creatures, they were formerly human.

The Festival of Hungry Ghosts, Yü Lan Hui (q.v.), is a time when kuei which have not yet been laid to rest can at least be appeased, lest they turn from wandering ghosts to malevolent demons.

Houses where some violent crime has been committed become haunted houses, *tsang fang*, and are believed to be uninhabitable for three years, as the ghostly resident is released if it can find another human to occupy its place within the allotted time. Ghosts, however, are afraid of blood, and by pricking the tip of the middle finger, they can usually be put to flight. The reason is that, like Dracula, they disappear at dawn, and dissolve into a pool of blood if struck by sunlight.

Ginseng The dried root of *Panax quinquifolia*, believed by the Chinese to possess magic powers on account of its resemblance to the human form. It only truly becomes efficacious after three hundred years, when it turns into a vegetative being with white blood, a few drops of which will restore a corpse to life. The age of the plant can be determined by its rings, as a tree. In Hong Kong, specialist pharmacies sell authenticated specimens, with certificates verifying the age and provenance. These fetch enormous sums, several thousand Hong Kong dollars being an acceptable price for a single specimen.

Goat see *Sheep*.

God of Happiness see *Fu Lu Shou*.

Gong-shu-zi see *Kung-shu Tzu*.

Great Bear The constellation of Ursa Major, the Great Bear, also known as the Dipper, is known to the Chinese as Pei Tou, the Northern Ladle. It is believed to be the home of Shang Ti (q.v.), the Emperor of the Gods, while certain stars are also the home of the Literary Genius, and the Mother of the Ladle, Tou Mu (q.v.).

In some legends, the seven major stars are celestial pigs, who draw the carriage of the Goddess of the Dawn, Chun T'i. Flags depicting the seven stars are often flown outside Taoist and Tibetan Buddhist monasteries. (See also *Pigs*.)

[Gu] Ku. See *Poison*.

Guan Di see *Kuan Ti*.

[Guan Yin] see *Kuan Yin*.

[Guan Gong] see Kuan Kung.

[Gui] see *Kuei*.

H

Huang Ti

Ha and Heng see *Heng Ha Erh Chiang*.

Han Hsiang-tzu The Sixth of the Eight Immortals (q.v.).

Han Shan Ta-shih see Han Shan Tzu in *Eighteen Lohan of Wu-wei*.

Han Yü AD 768–824, T'ang philosopher and poet. He stated that human nature is of three kinds: that in which goodness prevails, that which is evil, and that which is balanced. In AD 819 he remonstrated with the Emperor Hsien Tsung for the excessive reverence being paid to Buddhist relics. The Emperor was so enraged that he banished Han Yü to Canton [Guang Dong], at that time a country of savage barbarians, but Han Yü earned the respect and gratitude of the people and their descendants, for his extermination of a monstrous reptile which terrorized the area.

He was subsequently restored to office, and on his death canonized as Wen Kung. (See also *Eight Immortals*, sub entry for Han Hsiang-tzu.)

Hare see *Rabbit*.

Hell The concept of Hell was brought to China by the Buddhists. The early Chinese had a concept of Paradise, where those who became immortal would live, and even the most egregiously wicked villain could have some chance of immortality if they performed the correct rituals, or ingested the elixir of life (q.v.), hence, for an extreme example, the apotheosis of Chou Wang (q.v.).

Unlike Paradise, which was deemed to be distant and beyond the reach of ordinary mortals, Hell needed to be somewhere uncomfortably close; India was too remote to be threatening, and the infernal regions were therefore relocated in Szechüan.

A legend, which in all likelihood is founded on an actual incident, tells that Kuo, Governor of Szechuan (Ssu-ch'uan) during the reign of Shen Tsung (1573–1620), attempted to find the entrance to Hell. There being a large cave, or pothole, in a mountain at Feng-tu, he had himself lowered in a box, and later recorded his experience on a monument at Kuei-chou, in the north-east of Szechüan. There is no reason to doubt the account thus far, but whether he actually heard the cries of tortured souls below, or discovered an underground path which led from the temple at Feng-tu to a fine underground city with wide streets and a Hall of Justice is less certain.

In Hindu mythology, the Ruler of the Dead is Yama, which in Chinese becomes Yen-lo. In the classic Vedas he is merely the first man that died, and found the way to the eternal home, a place similar to the Greek Hades, or land of shades. But he is now seen as a terrifying judge of the dead. He is represented as green demon in red robes. He is attended by Ma Mien, Horse Face, and Niu T'ou, Ox Head, and the two ministers Wu Ch'ang (q.v.). These are all subservient to Ti Ts'ang Wang (q.v.), King of the Earth's Womb, who delivers the purgated souls from Hell and into the next reincarnation.

The soul of the departed has several obstacles to pass before it reaches the infernal regions. At the gate, demons demand money, and if none is forthcoming, they attack and beat the victim. Next the souls is weighed; the good are light, but the wicked are borne down by their evil and are punished. Next the soul arrives at Bad Dog Village, where the beasts are able to distinguish evil-doers from the innocent, and react accordingly. At the fourth stage, a mirror reveals the doom of reincarnation that awaits the sinner. Next the soul is taken to an observation post where it is allowed a final chance to see home and family, and ruefully cogitate on what might have been. At the sixth stage it is necessary to cross a vast chasm, the sinners having to cross it over a bridge only an inch wide, while the good souls pass over gold and silver bridges. At the seventh stage, the revolving wheel of the Law is reached, which ejects the soul into the form of its future incarnation, whether into the nobility, the deprived classes, or the animal kingdom. Before passing into their next existence, however, they are given a draught of refreshing liquor which wipes away all their previous experiences in the former life, and the purgation which followed.

Chinese almanacs graphically illustrate the punishments which await the perpetrators of various crimes. Those who are avaricious suffer the indignity of a *k'ang*: a wooden frame, attached to the neck like a portable pillory, on which the person's name and crimes are exhibited. This is the mildest of the punishments. Those who steal clothes from coffins are thrown into a mountain of fire, those who steal the actual bones are boiled in oil. Those who stir up enmity between relatives are gnawed by dogs and pigs, while those that make excess profits through printing books are impaled on spikes.

In Chinese, Hell is known as Ti Yü, the Earth Prison.

Heng Ha Erh Chiang Heng and Ha the two marshals; the Door Gods (q.v.). Historically, ministers of Chou Wang (q.v.), last emperor of the Shang (Yin) dynasty (*c.* 1121 BC).

The two marshals Cheng Lun and Ch'en Chi were known as Heng (the Snorter) and Ha (the Blower). Heng had received a magic power from the magician Tu O; when he snorted, it made a sound like a bell and two columns of light shot from his nostrils like laser beams, and had a similar destructive effect. Through this extraordinary human death ray, the wicked Chou Wang managed to win several victories, but he was eventually captured, and brought his powers to the opposing side.

Meanwhile, Chou Wang had another secret weapon. Ch'en Chi had learnt, from the same magician, how to blow out clouds of poisonous yellow gas. Ch'en Chi (Ha, the Blower) faced Cheng Lun (Heng, the Snorter) in a battle which was several thousands of years before its time, chemical warfare versus death ray. The poison gas seemed to be the dominant force until the Blower Ch'en Chi was wounded and killed by more conventional weapons: a bow and a spear. Cheng Lun (the Snorter Heng) was destroyed by an ox-spirit, who spat a bezoar stone in his face.

Heng and Ha are the guardians of the gates of Buddhist temples, and their pictures are often seen on their doorposts.

Heng O see *Ch'ang O.*

Ho Ch'ü-ping Died 117 BC. A commander in the army of the Han emperor Wu Ti (q.v.). In 121 BC he led an army to Karasha in Turkestan, and brought back a gold image which was worshipped there by the Hsiung-nu (the Huns). Some Chinese scholars are of the opinion (not universally supported) that the image was a Buddha, and was the first contact which China had with Buddhism.

Ho Ho Erh Hsien The Two Immortals Called Ho; patrons of merchants. Ho Ho (the two characters are different in Chinese) could be the name of one person, or as Ho and Ho, be the names of two. Ho Ho is usually represented as two people in popular pictures, as attendant on Tsai Shen, the God of Wealth.

Ho Ho (one person) was a native of Honan, born in AD 632. Wanting to find out news of his brother who had enlisted in the army, he made the return journey from Honan to Hsian and back, a distance of ten thousand *li* (3,333 miles), in one day. For this he was called Wan Hui (Ten Thousand Return).

Ho and Ho (two people) were Han Shan and Shih-teh. Han Shan seems to have been a disturbed vagrant, who attached himself to the monastery at Kuo-ching Ssu, but was not popular with the monks there owing to his mannerisms: gazing at the sky, cursing and shouting, and, when reproved, cackling with unseemly mirth. He was expelled from the monastery in AD 627, or, as is put more euphemistically, went into retreat nearby. He was last heard of in a cave in Han-yen.

Shih-teh, 'the Foundling' was raised at the Kuo-ching Ssu monastery. He took pity on Han Shan, and as Shih-teh worked in the kitchens, saved him scraps to feed him.

As Ho also means Harmony in Chinese, the popular notion is that Ho and Ho are the twin immortals of harmonious union.

Ho Hsien-ku The last in the list of the Eight Immortals (q.v.).

Horse The seventh animal of the Chinese zodiac (q.v.). (See also *Eight Horses; White Horse.*)

Horse Face Demon see *Hell; Ma Mien; Wu-Ch'ang Kuei.*

Hou I An archer in the service of the Emperor K'u (2436 BC) who shot down nine of the Ten Suns (q.v.); he also shot the Celestial Dog which devours the moon in times of eclipse.

Hou T'u, Lord of the Earth see *Earth God.*

Hsi-an [Xian] see *Ch'ang-an.*

Hsieh Hsü see *Lung Wang*.

Hsien An immortal. The Chinese character for Hsien consists of the two characters for Man and Mountain next to each other, signifying someone who lives on a mountain. The term is usually, but far from exclusively, reserved for Taoists who have attained immortality, which may be bestowed through good works, or obtained by taking the elixir of life. It is quite plain, from all accounts, that either way, becoming immortal did not lengthen one's life on the earth, but rather precipitated the departure from it.

Of all the Hsien, the most renowned are the Eight Immortals (q.v.) who are not only frequently portrayed in various art mediums, but are also the chief characters in an opera, Eight Immortals Crossing the Sea (q.v.), and other entertainments.

Hsien-yang Capital of China under its first emperor, Shih Huang-ti.

Hsi-ho According to the Shu Ching, the Book of Documents, there were three brothers called Hsi and three called Ho. The Emperor Yao ordered the brothers '. . . Hsi and Ho to calculate the disposition of the sun, moon, stars and planets, and so manifest the seasons to all men. He then ordered Younger Brother Hsi to stay with the Yü people at Yang Ku, and there to receive the rising sun, and order the works of the East. Then he ordered the Middle Brother Hsi to stay in the South, Chiao, there to attend to the solstice. Then he ordered Younger Brother Ho to stay in the West at Mei Ku, and pay respect to the departing sun, and regulate the autumn equinox. Then he ordered Middle Brother Ho to stay in the North at Yu Tu, there to attend to the winter solstice.'

According to other sources, Hsi-ho, unlike Ho Ho, is not two people masquerading as one, but one person, Hsi-ho, masquerading as six. He is either the charioteer of the Sun, or, in the Shan Hai Ching (q.v.), a female deity who gave birth to the Sun.

Hsi Men Pao A local magistrate, *c.* 410 BC, who deserves to be immortalized for ending the barbarous practice of sacrificing young girls to the Yellow River. The marriage of the River God was an annual ceremony presided over by a Wu, a shamaness or witch, and her retinue. The girl would be dressed in fine clothes, placed on a bed, and sent out onto the waves. Those families with beautiful daughters were either obliged to contribute to the upkeep of the temple, or move house, lest their daughter be selected to be the Dragon King's bride.

At last, Hsi Men Pao decided he wanted to attend the ceremony to give his respects to the bride. He asked the chief witch to fetch the girl for him to see, then declared that she was too ugly to become the Dragon King's bride, and ordered one of the witch's attendants to be thrown into the river, to tell the Dragon King that there was a delay. When no reply was brought back, he ordered the attendants to be thrown in one by one, until finally the chief witch herself was obliged to join the watery kingdom.

After that, the Dragon King made no more threats to the people living by the River.

Hsi Peh 1231–1135 BC. The title means 'Chief of the West'. He is more usually known by the name Wen Wang (q.v.) (the Literary King).

Hsi Shen The God of Joy. He is represented carrying a basket or sieve, on which there are three peachwood arrows (see *Peach*.) The picture is placed in front of a bride's sedan chair when she is being taken to her future home. Thuss, Hsi Shen seems to be a kind of Chinese cupid. He is sometimes shown being carried on the shoulders of the God of Wealth, or alternatively dressed in green, carrying gold ingots (q.v.).

The origin of Hsi Shen is unclear, and there is no tradition attached to his mortal or supernatural origins.

Hsi Wang Mu [Xiwang Mu] The Queen Mother of the West, one of the most important figures of Chinese mythology. She is revered today by women on reaching their 50th birthdays.

There are many legends woven round Hsi Wang Mu, and it is important to realize that legends in which Hsi Wang Mu is a central character do not mean that they are as old as the legend of Hsi Wang Mu herself. It is one thing to list the many traditional attributes and symbols associated with Hsi Wang Mu; it is quite another to identify those which are genuinely part of the Hsi Wang Mu legend.

The earliest reference is in the History of the Chou Dynasty, written in the second century BC, but compiled from earlier sources, which records that she entertained Mu Wang (q.v.) of the Chou dynasty in 985 BC, at a place known as the Lake of Gems. There are also references to the historic meeting in other classic texts, although these do not necessarily verify the account, since they may have used the same source as the History of the Chou Dynasty. Nevertheless, it does seem that she was originally a historic personage, the Queen of some distant western state. The accounts in subsequent legends of her meetings with earlier emperors, for example Fu Hsi, are now considered by many scholars to be later invention, introduced once Hsi Wang Mu had been culled from history and planted in the garden of mythology.

By the fifth century BC, some five hundred years after the encounter between Mu Wang and Hsi Wang Mu, the visit and entertainment had become the stuff of legend. The philosopher Lieh-tzu, of the fifth or fourth centuries, used the incident as the foundation for a number of allegorical stories, and introduced such elements of the legend as the K'un Lun Mountains, the Isles of P'eng-lai, and the Peaches of Immortality, although of course it is quite possible that these details were already current in folklore before Lieh-tzu committed them to paper. By the second century BC certain essential attributes of Hsi Wang Mu and associated elements of her supernatural court had been firmly established in the general imagination, as can be seen in the Banner of Ma Wang Tui (q.v.), which depicts Hsi Wang Mu together with the Hare and the Toad. It should be clear, now, that much of the substance of the legends which follow here will be, in Chinese historical terms, of comparatively late composition.

Hsi Wang Mu dwells on the K'un Lun mountains, in a palace made of pure gold, with walls one thousand *li* (333 miles) in circumference, and decorated with precious stones. Portraits usually depict her with two maids, one with a fan and the other with a basket of the peaches of longevity which grow in her garden. Five other girls in her retinue are the Jade Fairy Maids. She travels on a white crane, and a flock of bluebirds are her messengers. Her palace stands by the Lake of Jewels, (where she once entertained Mu Wang) and near it grow the fabulous peaches, taking three thousand years to form, and another three thousand to ripen.

When these become ripe, the Queen celebrates her birthday and gives a banquet at which the fruit is the chief delicacy served after dishes of bears' paws, monkeys' lips, dragons' livers and phoenix marrow.

The following legend is one of the older ones in which Hsi Wang Mu is a central figure.

Hou I (q.v.), the celestial archer, having shot down nine of the Ten Suns (q.v.), was asked by Hsi Wang Mu to build her a palace of jade in the Western sky. This he did successfully, and she rewarded him with a pill made from the peaches of immortality. However, he was instructed not to take the pill until he had fasted for one year. He hid the pill in the roof of his house, and for the next year he existed on the perfume of flowers. Unfortunately, his wife, Heng O, curious as to the source of a radiant light in the roof, found the pill, and swallowed it. Suddenly she felt herself floating, and fearful of her husband's return, she soared through the window. Hou I pursued her but she escaped him, and travelled to the Moon, where she was transformed into a three-legged toad.

With the toad sits the Hare, who sits under a cassia tree, distilling the elixir of life from another recipe.

Other legends concerning Hsi Wang Mu are nearly all of later date. Among the additional detail must be mentioned her consort, Tung Wang Kung, who may have been borrowed from Indian mythology. They had nine sons and twenty-four daughters.

Hsi Yu Chi (1); Hsi Yü Chi (2); Hsi Yu Chi (3) Records of a Journey to the West. There are two books called Hsi Yu Chi, and a third called Hsi Yü Chi, all of which may be called 'Records of a Journey to the West'. The first is a factual account, written by Li Chih-ch'ang, of a journey made by Ch'iu Ch'ang-ch'un to visit Jenghis Khan in Persia between 1221 and 1224.

The second book with a very similar title is an account of the authentic travels of the monk Hsüan Tsang (q.v.) to India, and his bringing back to China of the Buddhist scriptures. The third, which has the same title as the first mentioned book, is a fictional romance, loosely woven round the substance of the second, which introduces the Monkey King and his friend the Pig, popular characters in Chinese fiction. (See *Monkey King*.)

Hsüan Tan (Yüan Tan) see *Ts'ai Shen; Yüan Tan*.

Hsüan Tsang [Xuanzang] The religious name of T'ang Seng, a Buddhist monk (AD 602–64). The central character in the two works known as the 'Journey to the West', one fictional, the other documentary.

According to the official family history, his name was Ch'en, and he was born in Hou-shih, Loyang, in Honan. In 629 he petitioned the Emperor T'ai Tsung for permission to travel to India to bring back Buddhist books. On the Emperor's refusing he set out on his own. He travelled for sixteen years, visiting 130 kingdoms, and returned with a veritable library of the scriptures. On his return, he was summoned to the Palace, and given charge of the translation of the Hindu texts into Chinese. Before he died, he asked all present at his death-bed to call on the name Tz'u-shih Ju-lai. The following account is less austere in its treatment of factual matter.

In the reign of T'ai Tsung of the T'ang, Ch'en Kuang-jui took his university examinations, and obtained the highest mark. He married Wen-chiao, the daughter of Yin K'ai-shan, a government minister, and was appointed to the governorship of Chen-chiang in Kiangsu, and left his home to take up his position, his wife and mother accompanying him. Unfortunately, his mother fell sick on the journey, and they were obliged to rest a few days at the Inn of Ten Thousand Flowers. As she showed no sign of recovery, Ch'en was obliged to leave her there while he and his wife Wen-chiao travelled on to Chen-chiang. Before he left, he saw a fisherman with a fine carp, and thought it would make an ideal parting gift for his mother. But when he held the fish, he found it was still alive, and out of compassion he let it go. His mother was touched by her son's gesture, and promised him that his kindness would be rewarded some day.

Ch'en, Wen-chiao and a servant, returned to the river to take a boat to Chen-chiang. However, the boatman, Liu Hung, was smitten by Wen-chiao's beauty. That night, he moored the boat at a deserted spot, and murdered Ch'en and the servant. Then, armed with Ch'en's papers and official seal, he told Wen-chiao she had two options, silence or death. Wen-chiao, knowing that she was carrying her husband's child, chose silence. On arrival at Chen-chiang Liu Hung passed himself off as the new governor.

Soon the time came for Chen-chiang's confinement. Before the baby was born, however, the God of the South Pole came to her with a message from Kuan Yin (q.v.) to say that the child would be a son whose fame would resound throughout the empire. He also warned her that Liu Hung would kill the child if he could.

Fortunately, when the child was born, Liu Hung was away on business, so she took the child, wrapped it in a cloth, and took it to the bank of the Yangtze River. She wrote a note, in her own blood, giving the child's sad history, and, in case she should ever encounter the child again, bit off its left little toe as a permanent means of identification. A large piece of driftwood passing by provided her with the means for the child's transportation. She bound the child to it, and left it to the care of the elements.

The river carried the strange craft to the nearby monastery of Chin-shan Ssu. The child was rescued by an old monk, Chang Lao, and given the name of River-waif. The secret note was carefully preserved, and the child brought up as a monk, and when old enough to take his vows, given the religious name Hsüan Tsang.

Some years later, however, another young monk picked a quarrel with him, and mocked him for having neither father nor mother. Perplexed, Hsüan Tsang asked Chang Lao what the other monk meant. The old monk decided that the time had come to tell Hsüan Tsang the truth concerning his origins, and retrieved the note left by his mother. Incensed, the young monk decided he must avenge his murdered father, and in order to do this, left the monastery to become a wandering monk. Finding that his mother was still living with Liu Hung, he sent her a message, together with the cloth in which he had been wrapped as a child, and arranged to meet her at Chin Shan.

The mother, overwhelmed with emotion, gave her son the remaining details of the tale, and told him what he must now do. First he had to find his grandmother at the Inn of Ten Thousand Flowers, then travel on to Ch'ang-an, the capital, to give a letter to Wen-chiao's father, Yin K'ai-shan.

The grandmother was no longer at the Inn, having many years since despaired of ever hearing from the son who had apparently deserted her. She had become blind with weeping, and existed only on charity, living as a beggar by the city gate. Her grief was great at hearing of the terrible fate that had befallen her son, especially as she had repeatedly cursed him for abandoning her. But the arrival of the grandson was itself joy enough to restore her sight. Hsüan Tsang took her back to the Inn of Ten Thousand Flowers, saw her safely installed, then made his way with all speed to the capital.

Yin K'ai-shan read his daughter's letter with horror. He immediately despatched a report to the Emperor, who just as speedily ordered the arrest and execution of the murderous imposter. Yin K'ai-shan set off at once to rescue his daughter, arriving at the castle at night. The murderer was dragged from his bed, then taken to the spot where the crime had been committed. There the criminal was disemboweled, and his heart and liver sacrificed to appease the spirit of the murdered man.

Then a most bizarre thing happened. A body floated to the surface of the river. It was Hsüan Tsang's father, Ch'en. As the body reached the bank, it was apparent that Ch'en was still alive, and in the best of health. His murder all those years ago had been witnessed by the carp which he had returned to the water. It was no ordinary carp, however, but Lung Wang (q.v.), the Dragon King. In the intervening years Chen's spirit had been an officer at the Dragon King's court, but now that the sacrifice had appeased natural justice, it was time for the spirit to return to the terrestrial world. Ch'en and his son returned to Chen-chiang, where the father assumed the governorship to which he had been appointed eighteen years before.

The son returned to the capital, Ch'ang-an, where he became the Emperor's favourite religious counsellor. In the end, he was chosen to travel to the Western Paradise to receive the scriptures from Buddha in person. On his return he was rewarded by Milo the Buddhist, and made Controller of Rites to the Jade Emperor, Yü Huang (q.v.).

For more tales of Hsüan Tsang, see *Monkey King*.

Hsüan Tsung Emperor of the T'ang dynasty, reigned AD 713–56. He was an ardent follower of Taoism, and instituted colleges and schools for the study of the Tao. (See also *I-hsing; Tao.*)

Hu A witch or sorceress of the time of Emperor Wu Ti (q.v.). To the Chinese, she would have been regarded as a barbarian, being of the Hsiung-nu, or Hun, race. With a compatriot, Ch'iang Chung (q.v.), Wu Ti's personal guard, she plotted the destruction of Li, the heir apparent, by compounding a witch-hunt. (See also *Mu-jen.*)

Huai Nan Tzu [Apotheosis, 122 BC]; commonly called Huai Nan Tzu, the Prince of Huai Nan. Grandson of Liu Pang, founder of the Han dynasty, and nephew to the heirless Emperor Wu Ti (q.v.). Like his uncle, he gathered at his court a coterie of alchemists and magicians known as Fang Shih (q.v.). He was himself an ardent practitioner of the mystic arts, and author of the famous book on Taoist magic, Hung Lieh Chuan, 'The Vast and Eminent Chronicle', usually referred to simply as the Huai Nan Tzu. The Great Historian Ssu-ma Ch'ien says that he was implicated in a plot to succeed to the throne, was banished, and took his own life. Other sources, however, credit him with having success in distilling the elixir of life. On tasting it, he was suddenly transported to Heaven, and surprised by the unexpected flight, dropped the beaker which contained the essence. A few investigating dogs which lapped up the spilt dregs from the fallen goblet were borne aloft in a similar fashion.

A more elaborate version of events is given in the Shen-hsien t'ung-chien, 'The Complete Mirror of Spirits and Genie'. In the second century BC, a mysterious young man would appear every generation, giving his name as Wang Chung-kao. Being eventually introduced to King Liu An, he told the King that he was the brother of a former emperor who had lived two thousand years before, and was now teaching people the doctrine of immortality. When the king asked him how he could achieve immortality, Wang Chung-kao replied that he would be visited by his teachers.

In due course, after Wang Chung-kao had left the country, eight old men arrived, and asked to see the king. The king sent word that he desired three things: immortality, true knowledge, and the power to kill wild beasts, and that if they could offer him these, then he would see them. The old men said that these gifts were beyond the power of old men, and suddenly transformed themselves into young men. Hearing of the miracle, the king ran to fetch them to his palace, saying he would be their disciple. The immortals, as indeed they were, then assumed their original form of old men. The king began to study with them, learning the secrets of herbs and medicines, and how to prepare the elixir of life.

Now the king's son, Prince Liu Ch'ien, prided himself on his swordsmanship, and had challenged an officer, Lei Pei, to a contest. Unfortunately, Lei Pei injured the prince, and fearing for his life, plotted with a colleague, Wu Pei, to accuse King Liu An and his brother the King of Lu-chiang of planning a revolt against the Emperor, Wu Ti. When the King of Lu-chiang heard that the Imperial Messenger was on his way to arrest him, he hanged himself. But before the Messenger reached King Liu An, the Eight Immortals (q.v.) called on him, and urged him to follow them. When he heard of the treachery which had brought about his brother's death, his first reaction was to revenge himself on the two officers, but the Eight Immortals persuaded him that the taking of life was no path to immortality. The nine then gathered on a cloud, and set off towards the lands of the immortals, leaving behind the apparatus and medicines of their laboratory.

On arrival at the Heavenly Kingdom, the Eight Immortals warned Liu An to be respectful to all he met, but being formerly a king, he found it difficult to act with genuine humility, and kept referring to himself as king. As a result, Yü Ti (q.v.), the Jade Emperor, felt that Liu An was not ready to be accepted into the Immortal realm, and would have to be reincarnated. The Eight Immortals, however, recited his virtues, and given another chance, Liu An dropped his claim to being king, and took the humbler title of Huai Nan Tzu, the Philosopher of South Huai. That hurdle past, there remained only one more task. Huai Nan Tzu went with the Eight Immortals to the Western Sea where they found the corpse of his brother, King Lu-chiang. They prepared pills from the wood of the Soul Recalling Tree, placed these on the dead brother's lips, and brought him back to the living world to lead a life of virtue.

Huang Hsiang One of the most quoted of the Twenty-Four Examples of Filial Piety (q.v.). 'In summer he fanned his father's pillow, and in winter warmed his couch.'

Huang Ti The Yellow Emperor 2697 BC. In the records of Ssu-ma Ch'ien (q.v.) Huang Ti leads the Five Sovereigns (Wu Ti) who ruled at the dawn of time. Compilers of legends have added more detail; according to the Bamboo Annals he was miraculously conceived by his mother Fu Pao and born near the River Chi, from which he took his surname, and added the name Hsien Yüan, that being the name of a hill where he lived. But as Hsien Yüan also means 'wheeled vehicle' it was assumed that he invented them.

During his reign the stems-and-branches (q.v.) for reckoning time were instituted, astronomical instruments constructed and a calendar compiled. The system of twelve chromatic scales was devised, mathematical studies pursued, garments tailored, and objects of wood, metal and pottery manufactured. According to the Five Element theory (q.v.), his reign was influenced by the element Earth, whose symbolic colour is yellow.

The Feng-bird (phoenix) and the Ch'i-lin (unicorn) appeared at the close of his reign, signifying that it was a beneficent one.

Huang (a different Chinese character) also means Sovereign. The first Emperor of a united China combined Huang and Ti (Emperor) together to call himself Shih Huang Ti, the First Sovereign Emperor, although the title was not again in use until its readoption by the Manchus (Ch'ing dynasty) in the sixteenth century.

It is quite possible that the title of the ancient emperor Huang Ti (the Yellow Emperor) was actually a misreading for Huang Ti (Sovereign Emperor), as ancient texts frequently interchanged characters with the same or similar sounds. Bearing in mind that the Five Element (q.v.) theory was not conceived until several centuries after the time of the ancient emperor, it is not unthinkable that the association of the Yellow Emperor with the Earth element was due to a misunderstanding. (See also *Yü*.)

Huang Ku'n The patron of incense-makers. In the time of Emperor Yao (q.v.), lightning struck one of the trees in the Western Paradise, and a branch from it fell into a river. Its perfume was so sweet that it was presented to the Emperor, but only Huang K'un knew where it had come from.

Incense, in Chinese, is Hsiang, meaning perfume. Hong Kong (in Mandarin Chinese Hsiang Chiang) is sometimes translated as 'perfumed harbour' but the name is actually derived from a small port on the island which was renowned for its manufacture and distribution of incense.

Huang Ta Hsien see *Wong Tai Sin*.

Huang T'ing Chien 1045–1105. Celebrated poet, one of the Twenty-Four Examples of Filial Piety (q.v.).

Human spirit The following is a resumé of the belief concerning death and afterlife prevailing during the Han dynasty, which formed the basis of subsequent Taoist doctrine.

The physical form of a person is the *Hsing*; *p'o* keeps the body alive, and *hun* is the conscious mind. *P'o* and *hun* separate at death, but for various reasons, perhaps to avenge a murder, or to right a wrong, they may remain together and inihabit some other body. Spiritually higher beings are also more likely to keep the *p'o* and *hun* united for a longer period after death.

When the *p'o* and *hun* separate, the *hun*, after leaving the body through the fontanelle, has the opportunity to rise to the abodes of the blessed, but does not always achieve this ultimate aim. The *p'o* stays with the corpse, however (three years according to some Taoist authorities), provided that the proper funeral offerings are made. But should this fail, the *p'o* turns into a *kuei*, or ghost, often malevolent. After a decent interval, the *p'o* goes to the Yellow Springs, a kind of purgatory. To ease its existence there, and to prevent it being disenchanted and returning to earth as a *kuei*, it is provided with the necessities for the next world in the tomb. To this day, traditional Chinese funerals include the ritual of burning elaborately constructed paper models of houses, cars, games tables, clothes and even Hell money to provide the material comforts in the Yellow Springs. In Han times, clay models, and even actual domestic items were buried with the deceased, while in earlier times a powerful ruler would also have his entire household executed and buried with him to wait on him in the next world.

To keep the *p'o* in the body for as long as possible, the body's mouth and other orifices were stopped with pieces of precious jade, and in the case of the wealthiest, the entire corpse was completely clad in a suit of jade pieces sewn together with solid gold wire.

As for the *hun*, the road to Paradise is so perilous that unless the deceased was a person of high rank or someone very spiritual, it would have very little chance of reaching its goal. Poetry of the third century BC reveals that it was customary to try to dissuade the *hun* from embarking on the hazardous adventure, and return to its body to die a second death. If, however, the soul could not be persuaded to abandon its quest, then a cosmological map of the next world would be a useful addition to the funerary furnishings. (See also *Hell; Paradise; Vampires.*)

Hun The conscious soul. See *Human spirit*.

Hungry Ghosts Festival see *Yü Lan Hui*.

Hun T'un Hun T'un, meaning Chaos, occurs in a number of different versions of the Creation myth, but in widely different guises. In human form, Hun T'un is said to be a wicked son of the Yellow Emperor (q.v.), sent into exile either by his father, or the Emperor Shun (q.v.). According to the Shan Hai Ching (q.v.), Hun T'un is a bird like a yellow bag, though its colour is the red of fire; it has no face, but has six feet and four wings — which might suggest that it was not so much a bird as a butterfly. Another source from the fourth century BC says that in ancient times, the Emperor Hu of the Northern Sea, and Emperor Shu of the Southern Sea would meet and confer at the court of Emperor Hun T'un of the Centre (in Chinese, 'Centre' can also mean China). Emperor Hun T'un was only partly formed, lacking the seven orifices for hearing, seeing, scenting, and tasting. The two visitors therefore decided to repay their host's hospitality by boring the required orifices, one each day. Alas, on the seventh day, Hun T'un died, and at the same moment the Earth was created. The story is intriguing because it suggests a seven-day creation, echoing Genesis. Chinese calendars did not recognize a seven-day week until a thousand years later.

See also *Tao Cosmology*.

Huo Pu, Minister of Fire see *Elements, the Five*.

I

I Ching

I Ching (Yi Jing) The Book of Changes; also known as the Chou I, the (Book of) Changes of the Chou Dynasty. One of China's most ancient works of literature, and regarded as a sacred text, even being a required book for the official examinations at one period. (See *Tao*.) Unlike other sacred books of China, which have their parallels in the chronicles, psalms, legal and moral works of the Bible, the I Ching has no Western equivalent. It is a heterogenous compilation of brief utterances, some no longer than a few characters, which are regarded as the medium through which Heaven can make its will known.

The I Ching consists of sixty-four sections, each headed by a diagram of six lines, which may be solid or broken. (See *Eight Diagrams*.) The diagrams, chosen through a random process of throwing sticks, each have a name or title which gives a clue to its interpretation, such as 'Poison' or 'Not Yet Finished'. In many cases the title is followed by a short mystical verse, although often there is merely a terse statement to say whether the diagram indicates good fortune or not. Following the title and its verse, a second text refers to the individual lines of the diagrams.

The title, its verse, and the text for the lines comprise the main body of the I Ching. The text for the title and its verse is usually attributed to Wen Wang (q.v.), and that for the lines by his son Wu Wang (q.v.), founder of the Chou dynasty, and though this may be invention, there are astronomical clues in the 'lines' text which apparently confirm that they were written at the time of the Chou dynasty.

Although Confucius (born 551 BC) is supposed to have said, 'If I could add years to my life, I would dedicate them all to a study of the I Ching,' it is doubtful that he ever encountered the work. It is not mentioned by the Grand Historian Ssu-ma Ch'ien, born in 145 BC, although it was well known to the philosopher Yang Hsiung, born in 53 BC. The pithy phrases which form the text to the diagrams themselves seem to be the oldest text, and may be the last vestiges of a shamanist oral tradition which has now disappeared. The text for the lines appears to be more refined and of a later date.

Recent archaeological evidence has revealed variant forms of the I Ching that were current in first and second centuries BC, and shows that there was no standard version either for the names of the diagrams, nor for the order in which they appeared. This may account for the unusual name Chou I: Book of Changes of the Chou, meaning a version that was used by the Chou family, or dynasty, perhaps, as distinct from other books of changes. Translations and adaptations of the I Ching as they exist today are based on an authorized version prepared many centuries later. (See also *Poison*.)

I-hsing, Ch'an-shih AD 672–717. I-hsing the Ch'an (Zen) scholar, monk, astronomer, and mathematician, the author of several astronomical treatises. He is credited with a marvellous memory, being able to recite long documents after a single reading. Emperor Hsüan Tsung (q.v.) was so impressed that he addressed him as Prophet. He is also remembered for the following moral tale.

Although he was of good family, he was nevertheless poor, and a widow named Wang-mu supported him during his student years. It so fell out that years later, when I-hsing had influence at court, the widow's son was found guilty of manslaughter, and sentenced to execution. Wang-mu approached I-hsing to ask him to intercede for her son, but he admitted that although he owed her a great debt of gratitude, he could not extend his influence beyond what was just. She began to curse him for his torpidity, but he eventually reassured her that the son would be saved.

He went to a nearby temple, and rented a room there, where he placed a large jar. He called a temple attendant, and swearing him to secrecy, told him that on a certain day, at a precise time, seven animals would come into the garden. The attendant was to make sure he caught every one of them and put them in a bag. At the appointed time, seven pigs ran into the garden, and the attendant duly caught them, and popped them into the bag. The attendant brought the pigs to I-hsing, who rewarded the man for his efforts and put the pigs into the jar. I-hsing then sealed the jar with a wooden lid and wrote some mystic Indian characters in vermilion ink on the top. No one, of course, could guess the true purpose of the monk's strange actions. The next day, however, the Imperial Astronomer reported that the seven major stars of the Great Bear had disappeared. This being an omen of grave portent, Emperor Hsüan Tsung called I-hsing and asked his advice. The monk replied that it was indeed a dreadful omen and that to bring back the missing stars it would be best to grant a general amnesty to all prisoners. The Emperor agreed, and each day one of the little pigs was released. As a consequence, the stars reappeared one by one. By the end of the week, the constellation was restored, the widow's son was released, and no one was any the wiser.

Three points in the above story are worth noting. The Emperor Hsüan Tsung was a fervent Taoist, and a general amnesty was declared at one time, to secure the recovery of the Empress. The seven pigs, representing the seven major stars of the Great Bear, are usually shown accompanying the goddess Chun T'i (q.v.). The circumstances of I-hsing's death were carefully recorded. An official called Fei K'uan, a Buddhist, had presented himself to the old teacher of I-hsing, a certain P'u-chi, for tuition. One day, P'u-chi excused himself in the middle of a discussion, saying that he had been called away, then went to a temple, lit some incense and began to pray. After a while, a voice announced, 'The Grand Master I-hsing has arrived.' The monk approached P'u-chi, and whispered a few words, then after bowing three times, left. P'u-chi summoned the disciples and told them to toll the bells of the monastery, as I-hsing was departing for the Western Paradise. When they entered the hall, they found I-hsing dead. He was buried with great honour, and given the posthumous title Ta-hwei Ch'an-shih, Highly Intelligent Scholar of Zen. (See also sub-entry for Ts'ao Kuo-chiu under *Eight Immortals*.)

Immortals, The Eight see *Eight Immortals*.

Imperial Encyclopaedia The common name for the monumental work, Ku-chin T'u-shu Chi-ch'eng, the All-Embracing Illustrated Volumes of Things Then and Now. It was begun in the mid eighteenth century during the reign of the K'ang Hsi Emperor (reigned 1662–1723), and was intended to be a record of all human knowledge. When eventually completed, it comprised over ten thousand volumes, forty of them needed for the table of contents alone. It was the world's greatest typesetting feat, yet it is doubtful if more than thirty copies were printed. Today, only one complete copy exists outside China, in the British Library. Adding to the work's unparalleled rarity is the fact that as each section was printed, the whole fount was melted down for coinage.

Ingots Chinese gold ingots have a distinctive shape, something like a hat or paper boat. They feature prominently on lucky pictures, and are associated with the God of Wealth. Large gilt boxes in the shape of ingots are considered to be lucky presents, and are sometimes used by those fortune-tellers who do not make a fixed charge to hold the donations of their clients.

I Ti The inventor of wine. Little is known of this benevolent sage, other than that in the Chan Kuo Ts'e, Annals of the Warring States (480–403 BC) there is a passing remark: 'The Emperor's daughter commanded I Ti to make wine, and it was good. She gave it to Yü, but when he had tasted it, he poured it on the ground, sent I Ti to banishment, and forbade all knowledge of wine.' But unfortunately it is not clear just who Yü, the Emperor, his daughter, or I Ti, actually were.

J

Hsi Wang Tu with Jade Maidens

Jade The Chinese word Yü applies to a number of hard stones, and at least two different minerals with similar physical properties are identified as jade. The colour, which need not be the dark green usually associated with the mineral, and the variegation of the pattern in the stone determine its value as much as its hardness, precious jade being valued more highly than gold or diamonds of equal weight.

Jade was considered to bestow immortality; it was believed that jade emerged from the mountains as a liquid (which is in fact the case) and solidifies after ten thousand years. Mixed with the correct herbs, it returns to its liquid state (alas, not yet proven) and produces a draught which may be taken as the elixir of life. It was also considered to have the power of preserving the *p'o* (q.v.) and increasing the chances of immortality. Pieces of jade would be placed into the orifices of the body; and a jade disc, the *pi*, would be placed over the heart. In the celebrated burial at Ma Wang Tui (q.v.), the bodies were completely encased in suits of jade.

Taken in pill form, if not actually conveying immortality, it could endow the user with the power of levitation. Jade is also a talisman against being thrown from a horse.

Jade Emperor see *Yü Huang*.

Jade Maidens Attendants on Hsi Wang Mu (q.v.).

Jan-teng Fo (Jan-teng the Buddhist, to distinguish him from the following entry.) The Lamp Bearer; a Buddhist saint. The origins of the saint and the name are obscured by the number of competing versions of his biography. Jan-teng was variously:

1. A beggar woman from She-wei, intrigued by the fact that rich people presented offerings to the Buddha, resolved to save enough to buy some oil for one of the lamps. The temple caretaker, whose function was to extinguish the lamps at night, found that this lamp refused to go out. Subsequently the beggar woman became a Buddhist nun, and was reborn as a Buddha.
2. The teacher of Sakyamuni in a previous incarnation. When he was reborn, a number of bright lights mysteriously appeared round his cradle, this being the reason for his name.
3. Again, the teacher of Sakyamuni, but as a Taoist (see the next entry). Sakyamuni, having failed to become enlightened, set out to China to study with Jan-teng at Liang Shan, and understood the whole of Taoist perfection in thirteen days, after which he returned to India to teach the Way.
4. The hermit Lao-tu-po-t'i, a Brahman who had converted a thousand persons of high rank, all living as anchorites. One day, a *yaksha*, or beneficial genie, requested their hearts and blood to feed on. Only Lao-tu-po-t'i complied, and thus attained Buddhahood as Jan-teng, but the thousand kings were obliged to wait until the end of the *kalpa* (great age) of stability until they could become the Thousand Buddhas of the present time.
5. A Taoist. See the following entry.

Jan-teng gave Li Ching, one of the Eight Immortals (q.v.) the pagoda he carries in his left hand.

Jan-teng Tao-ren Jan-teng the Taoist, obviously intended to distinguish him from Jan-teng Fo. In the Battle of the Ten Thousand Spirits, he slaughtered Tou Mu, the Mother of the Pole Star by striking her with a pearl. He also trapped Yin Chiao, son of Chou Wang, between two mountains.

Jen Huang The name commonly given to T'ien-ying, eldest of the sons of Tou Mu, when he became a human king. See *Chun T'i*.

Jen [Ren] Mankind. See *Human spirit.*

Jen Wang Human Kings, the Nine Sons of Tou Mu. See *Chun T'i.*

Journey to the West A popular work of Chinese fiction, loosely based on the actual travels of the monk Hsüan Tsang (q.v.) to India to fetch the Buddhist scriptures. (See *Monkey King.*) There are two other famous Chinese books, one with the same and another with a similar title, noted under the entry *Hsi Yu Chi.*

Ju-i [Ruyi] A kind of sceptre, originally a sword guard of iron, and of a distinctive curved shape, something like a three-dimensional question mark. They were subsequently made of jade and other attractive or precious materials. The shape is said to be reminiscent of the fungus of long life, and presentation *ju-i* are regarded as appropriate gifts, conferring the wish that the recipient may live a long and happy life.

In Buddhist symbolism, the *ju-i* signifies the doctrines.

Ju Shui Literally, Weak Water. The P'eng-lai Isles were surrounded by weak water which could not support a swimmer or boat; consequently it was only possible to reach them by air, as only immortals could.

K

Ka-li-ha

Ka-li-ha, Kala see Chia-li-chia in *Lohan, The Eighteen*.

Kao, The Two Brothers Kao Ming and Kao Chio were known as
Ch'ien-li Yen 'Thousand Li Sight' and Shun-feng Erh, 'Favourable
Wind Ears'. Kao Ming was tall and blue-faced, with piercing eyes, a
large mouth and prominent teeth; his brother Kao Chio had a green
face, two horns, a red beard and a large mouth with sword-like teeth.
Naturally they found favour with Chou Wang (q.v.), and were
despatched by him to do battle with the armies of Wu Wang (q.v.) at
the Battle of Mu (q.v.).

Their first test was with Li No-cha (q.v.), whose magic bracelet was
ineffective. Chiang Tzu-ya (q.v.) thought it prudent to consult the I
Ching (q.v.), and discovered that it was only necessary to smear them
with the blood of a chicken and a dog to destroy their magic power.
This information, however, was of no use to them, because Thousand
Li Sight and Favourable Wind Ears had already seen and heard
everything. However, it was conveyed to Chiang Tzu-ya that the two
brothers were actually a peach-tree and a pomegranate tree, and that
the spirits had taken residence in two images at a temple of Huang

Ti (q.v.). By rooting up the trees and destroying the images, the power of the brothers would be erased. In order that the brothers did not learn of the plan, the soldiers were ordered to wave red flags, and beat drums and gongs, and under cover of the racket, the plan was discussed. When next they went to attack Chiang Tzu-ya's forces, they found that they were powerless, and were quickly despatched by one blow of Chiang Tzu-ya's scourge.

Kao-yao [gao-yao] The Magistrate in the time of the legendary Emperor Shun, who used the services of the unicorn (q.v.) to determine right from wrong.

K'eng San Ku-niang The Three Lavatory Ladies. It was formerly customary to offer as a wedding present a red bucket for use as a water closet, and also for the delivery of children. The euphemism for the bucket is Golden Bushel of Troubled Origins. When used for its more salubrious purpose, it was guarded by three female immortals. They were sisters of one Chao Kung-ming, who had fought on the side of Chou Wang (q.v.) in the epic battle against King Wu. The brother was killed in the battle, and the three sisters attempted to avenge his death by throwing their Golden Bushel of Troubled Origins at the enemy. After the opposing side had proved victorious, however, Chiang Tzu-ya recognized their valour, and canonized them by appointing them to supervise childbirth.

Kitchen God see *New Year Customs; Tsao Chün.*

Ko Hung Fourth century AD. Author of treatises on the transmutation of metals, the preparation of the elixir of life (q.v.), and the Shen Hsien Chuan, Biographies of Spirits and Immortals, the latter work being a prime source of information on Chinese legendary figures. He is also credited by some authorities as being the originator of the P'an Ku myth (q.v.), though this is doubtful. The patron of dyers.

Ku [Gu] see *Poison.*

Kuan Kung [Guan Gong] Also Kuan Yü. God of War; see *Kuan Ti.* Sometimes called the God of Riches. See *Ts'ai Shen.*

Kuan Ti [Guan Di], Kuan Yü Also Kuan Yü, Kuan Kung, Wu Ti. AD 162–220. A seller of bean-curd who went on to study. His name was originally Chang. After his parents had shut him up in a room for a punishment, he broke out, and killed a magistrate who was Kuan forcing his attentions on a young girl. He fled, and finding that he was not recognized, changed his name to Kuan. On his travels, he struck up a friendship with two others, and formed an alliance known as the Brothers of the Peach Orchard, a Chinese version of the Three Musketeers.

He was celebrated as one of China's finest military heroes, and was elevated to the rank of God of War in 1594. As such he became one of the most popular deities of China. His worship is not confined to the military, for although his portrait was to be found everywhere in military establishments, he was also invoked to aid anyone needing assistance. Because of his earliest calling, he is the patron of bean-curd sellers.

Curiously, he is also one of the patrons of literature, because from his student days he learned to recite the whole of the Commentary on the Spring and Autumn Annals by heart.

His holy days are the fifteenth day of the second moon, and the thirteenth day of the fifth.

Kuan Yin [Guan Yin] The Chinese form of Avalokita: the one who hearkens to the sound. A highly revered manifestation of the Buddha, and one of the forms most frequently encountered in Central Asia and China. Avalokita, originally Avalokitesvara, 'The Lord who Regards', was first described in the Lotus Sutra, and is a late addition to the Buddhist scriptures. This chapter first appeared in Chinese between AD 384 and 417. By the T'ang dynasty, Avalokitesvara was usually, but not exclusively, represented in paintings and sculpture as a female deity, and given the less barbaric sounding name of Kuan Yin. The unusual transformation can be explained by the fact that Avalokita had the power to assume whatever form was necessary to alleviate suffering, and the guise of a young woman was usually the most effective one to convey sympathy and compassion. The imagery parallels the Madonna of Christian belief.

Kuan-yu see *Kuan Ti.*

Kubla Khan, Khubilai, K'u-pi-lai (1215–94). Grandson of Jenghis Khan, and founder of the Yüan or Mongol dynasty. Among his achievements were the spread of Buddhism at the expense of Taoism, though he tolerated other religions. Other innovations introduced during his reign were the Mongolian alphabetic script, the revision of the calendar (1280) and the distribution of paper money (in 1285). Less successful were his attempts to extend the Empire to Indochina and Japan. In 1274, he received Marco Polo, who brought to the West many

of the first fabulous accounts of China and its customs. He was said
to have been buried with no monument, but claims to the discovery
of his tomb in the Gobi desert have happily coincided with the recent
independence of Mongolia. He was canonized as Shih Tsu. (See also
Xanadu.)

Kuei [Gui] (a) Ghost: see *Human spirit*; (b) Tortoise: see *Celestial
Emblems*.

K'uei The Literary Star. See *Wen Ch'ang*.

Kuei Ku-tzu A legendary minister at the court of Huang Ti (q.v.). He
was commissioned to continue the medical treatise on herbalism
attributed to Shen Nung (q.v.). He was reincarnated as the Patron of
Fortune-Tellers in the fourth century BC, and is also credited with the
invention of spectacles.

K'un Lord of Ts'ung, father of Yü the Great (q.v.). In 2297 BC, the
Emperor Yao (q.v.) ordered him to drain the floodwaters from the
country, but though he laboured for nine years, he failed. He was
banished, and the task passed to his son.

Kung Kung One of the most ancient figures of Chinese mythology,
mentioned in the Shan Hai Ching (q.v.). A supposed minister in the
time of the Emperor Yao, he was in charge of Water Courses, but failed
to prevent floods and was consequently banished. In other accounts,
he was the leader of a battle of the gods, and threatened to destroy
the earth with floods. In either case, he is considered to be the God
of Water. Kung Kung's main contribution to the present structure of
the universe was knocking his head on the Imperfect Mountain, which
caused the earth to tilt. (See also *Creation; Nü Kua*.)

Kung-shu Tzu [Gong-shu Zi] see *Lu Pan*.

K'un Lun (Kwen Lun) A mountain of Central Asia, identified with
the Hindu Kush. In the oldest classics, it is merely described as a place
where wild people of the west brought felt cloth and skins for sale and
barter, but later the mountain became regarded as the central pillar
of the world, supporting the heavens. Being the ladder between this
world and the next, all tales of marvels and miraculous beings were
obliged to mention K'un Lun somewhere in the narrative.
    According to the Shan Hai Ching (q.v.), the Book of Mountains and
Oceans, it was 3,300 miles in circumference, and 4,000 miles high. At

its base flowed the Blue, Black, White and Red rivers, the river of the
fifth colour, Yellow (q.v.), flowing through central China. It is the home
of Hsi Wang Mu (q.v.), and according to Huai Nan Tzu (q.v.), its slopes
were in neat terraces; the fields of grain, coriander and sesame in
abundance were a beautiful sight; there were trees of pearls, jade and
other precious stones. The Cinnabar streams circle it three times, and
those who drink it escape death. The Yellow River (according to Huai
Nan Tzu) flows from it, while the Ju Shui (q.v.), Weak Water, flows from
a hollow. Other marvellous features of the mountain have been shown
to be importations from Hindu mythology. One potent clue is the
statement in the Shih I Chi, Records of Officials of the T'ang Dynasty,
that an alternative name for K'un Lun was Mount Sumeru, in Hindu
mythology the residence of the god Indra and his consort. While Hsi
Wang Mu may be an indigenous Chinese goddess, the concept of the
dual figures of Hsi Wang Mu (Queen Mother of the West) and her
consort Tung Wang Kung (The King of the East) is a much later
addition to the mythology, and was almost certainly imported from
India with the advent of Buddhism.

Kuo Governor of Szechuan. See *Hell*.

Kuo Ch'ü Second century. In dire poverty, he had a wife and child
to support, as well as his mother. He therefore decided to bury the
child so that they would have enough food to feed them all. As he and
his wife were digging the pit for the child's grave, they found a gold
ingot inscribed with the words 'A gift from Heaven to Kuo Ch'ü'. One
of the Twenty-Four Examples of Filial Piety (q.v.).

L

Lao Tzu

La Festival A sacrifice offered to all the deities, spirits and immortals, three days after the winter solstice. The festival was instituted by the Ch'in Emperor, Shih Huang Ti (q.v.) (249–206 BC). It is now held on the eighth day of the twelfth month, and is marked by a special meal, a porridge or gruel made of five grains (rice, barley, wheat, corn and millet) representing the five elements, to which a number of other vegetables and fruits are added. Another version is that the porridge should have the five tastes: sweet, sour, salty, bitter, acid and hot, or contain the five spices: salt, vinegar, ginger, garlic and pepper. It is believed to ward off disease, evil spirits and the cold if eaten on that particular day.

Lake of Gems The place where Hsi Wang Mu (q.v.) entertained the Emperor Mu, according to the History of the Chou Dynasty.

Lantern Festival Fifteenth day of the first lunar month, approximately the end of February, when the Moon is full. The celebrations are said to be in honour of the approach of spring and lengthening days, coupled with prayer for rains. During the Han dynasty, it was the occasion for sacrifices to T'ai I, the God of the Pole Star, because he embodied the two principles of Yin and Yang. But by the fifth century AD, the religious aspect seems to have disappeared, and the festival became an occasion for poetic contests, the lanterns being decorated with pithy verses.

Emperor Yang Ti of the Sui dynasty (AD 581–618) marked the Lantern Festival with elaborate and costly entertainments with 3,000 actors and 18,000 musicians taking part in theatrical performances on stages that stretched for three miles.

Today, celebrations mostly take the form of theatricals, outdoor games and sports, fireworks, and, of course, splendid illuminations by lanterns which can be made from a variety of materials, but mostly paper.

Lan Ts'ai-ho The Seventh of the Eight Immortals (q.v.).

Lao Lai Tzu Chou dynasty. One of the Twenty-Four Examples of Filial Piety (q.v.). Even when 70, he still looked after his parents, and to entertain them in their dotage, he would dress up in fantastic costumes to dance and clown about.

Lao Tzu Lao Chün, Lao Tan; The Old Philosopher. Born 604 BC, hence contemporary with, but older than, Confucius (q.v.).

According to Ssu-ma Ch'ien (q.v.) his official name was Li Erh, he was born in Honan, and held the post of keeper of the records at Loyang, then the Chou dynastic capital. He is said to have discussed his philosophy of the Tao (q.v.) with Confucius, though the meeting is probably an invention.

The circumstances of his passing are not recorded. He is said to have retired to a place beyond the western frontiers about 500 BC, which would have put his age at that time at 96.

With the growth of Taoism, and its transformation into a mystical rather than philosophical religion, many legends were woven round his supposed activities. But despite legends which say, among other things, that Lao Tzu was born in 1321 BC from his mother's left side after a confinement lasting eighty years, and that when born he had snowy hair and a long white beard, there is not a shred of the supernatural in Lao Tzu's own writings, the Tao Teh Ching, which are pre-eminently philosophical and moral.

Lao Tzu is usually depicted as an old man riding a buffalo.

Lavatory Ladies, The Three see *K'eng San Ku-niang*.

Lei Chen-tzu One of the sons of Thunder (Lei) who was hatched from an egg after a thunderclap and found by the soldiers of Wen Wang (q.v.). The king adopted him, but as he already had ninety-nine children, he gave the child to Yün Chung-tzu, one of the sons of the Clouds, to bring up. When Wen Wang was taken prisoner by Chou Wang (q.v.), Lei Chen-tzu found two apricots and ate them, after which wings grew on his back, his face turned green, his nose became long and pointed, tusks grew from his jaw, and his eyes shone like mirrors. He now went to the rescue of Wen Wang, bringing his adoptive father home on his back.

Lei Hai-ch'ing Patron deity of musicians, usually depicted with four musician attendants. He became a god as the result of an unfortunate practical joke. He lived during the time of the Five Dynasties, hence his sobriquet, Wu-tai, Yüan-shih, Marshal of the Five Dynasties.

Lei Hai-ch'ing was a musician; while he was taking a nap, some school-friends drew a crab on his face, and put two willow branches behind his ears, the word 'crab' in the local dialect sounding like 'hai', and the willow branches being green (ch'ing in Chinese), they represented his name. When he awoke, he was so distraught that he committed suicide.

The worship of the spirit is somewhat alarming. The image is placed on an altar, its forehead dabbed with vermilion, and candles and incense burnt. Then the priests dance as if possessed, scratch their tongues, and write messages with the blood. Afterwards, the musicians, who also act as diviners, interpret the messages.

Lei Tsu The Ancestor of Thunder; the apotheosis of Wen-chung T'ai-shih (q.v.). He has three eyes, one in the middle of his forehead which emits a laser-like beam, and for transport he rides on a black unicorn which travels at the speed of light.

Wen Chung, defeated in the Battle of Mu (q.v.), retreated to Yen Shan, the Swallow Mountain, and encountered Ch'ih Ching-tzu, who flashed his Yin–Yang (q.v.) mirror at his unicorn, and overpowered it. One of Wu Wang's marshals, Lei Chen-tzu (q.v.), struck the animal with his staff and split it in two. Wen Chung escaped to Chüeh-lung Ling, but was barred by another of Wu Wang's marshals, Yün Chung-tzu. Using his hands to produce lightning, Yün Chung-tzu produced eight columns of fire which surrounded and imprisoned Wen Chung until he was burnt out of existence.

After the battle, Chiang Tzu-ya (q.v.) and Yüan-shih canonized him as Lei Tsu, giving him the direction over thunder, clouds and rain.

Lei Tsu is the patron deity of Seedsmen, Cornchandlers and

Innkeepers, some adding to his duties the making of cakes and even silk-weaving. To tread on rice and crush it underfoot is considered very bad luck, incurring the wrath of Lei Tsu, who strikes the offender with a lightning bolt. His holy day is the twenty-fourth of the sixth moon.

Li A Chinese measure of distance, about a third of a mile. Where the present text gives distances such as 33 miles, 3,300 miles, and so on, the original text would have stated a hundred or ten thousand *li*— in most cases probably an approximation and exaggeration. The term *li* has been retained, however, when the sense would otherwise be obscure, as in the name of Li Pa-pai (q.v.).

Li Ching T'o-t'a Li, the Pagoda Bearer. A general who fought with Wu Wang (q.v.) against Chou Wang (q.v.). His son, Li No-cha (q.v.) brought disgrace on the family by killing the envoy of Lung Wang (q.v.), the Dragon King.

As a result of the eventual reconciliation between father and son, he was given a golden pagoda. He is depicted holding a model of it. According to other sources, he was originally the Hindu god of thunder, but Chinese artists mistook the shape of a thunderbolt for a pagoda.

Li No-cha Third son of Li Ching (q.v.). A popular figure in Chinese romance, said in one to be sixty feet tall, with three heads, nine eyes, eight hands each with a golden weapon, and the ability to spew out blue clouds. At his voice the earth shook and demons trembled.

No-cha was born in a miraculous way. His mother Yin-shih had a fever and dreamt that a Taoist priest came into her room. Astounded, she scolded him for his temerity, but he said, 'Woman, receive the child of the Unicorn.' She awoke in fright, and told her husband. But immediately she felt the pain of childbirth. Her husband left her with her women, apprehensive about the significance of these strange events, when suddenly the maidservants rushed back and announced that his wife had given birth to a monster.

He ran to the bedchamber, but was astonished to see it filled with red light and a peculiar smell. In the middle of the room a ball of flesh was spinning, emitting a red glow. He took his sword and cut the ball open, and in it was a baby. It was wearing luminous red silk trousers and a gold bracelet, both of which belonged to the Taoist priest, Chin-kuang Tung, whom the wife had seen in her dream. The priest called to see the child, and announced that his name was No-cha.

One hot day, when No-cha was 7 years old and already six feet tall, he went to bathe in a stream. The incandescent trousers made the

stream boil, which caused the foundations of the Dragon King's palace
to shake. The Dragon King, Lung Wang (q.v.), sent a messenger to find
the cause of the trouble, and seeing the boy, spoke to him roughly and
made as if to carry him off. No-cha, however, threw the gold bracelet
at him and killed him. The incident was the cause of all the subsequent
battles between No-cha and various other emissaries of the Dragon
King, and later, between No-cha and his father Li Ching.

On the eventual reconciliation Li Ching was made an Immortal.

Li Pa-pai An immortal said to have lived from the end of the Hsia
to the beginning of the Chou dynasties, 800 years in all. His name
Li means 'plum' and is a common Chinese surname; Pa-pai means
'eight hundred'. But as Li is a homonym for *li*, the Chinese measure
of distance, Li Pa-pai sounds like eight hundred *li*, which he is said
to have walked every day. However, the bizarre anecdote for which he
is most renowned neither occurs during his supposed lifetime nor has
anything to do with his ability to walk great distances.

In the time of the rebel emperor Wang Mang (AD 6–8), Li called on
a certain official, T'ang Kung-fang (q.v.) to be the official's teacher and
adviser. When he arrived, Li's body was covered in boils, which he
claimed could only be cured by someone licking them clean. The
official ordered his servants to perform this noisome cure, but it had
no effect because it had to be done by someone of noble birth. T'ang
therefore licked the sores himself. Unfortunately, this was ineffective,
so T'ang's wife was obliged to perform the same odious task. That also
failing, Li announced that it was now necessary for him to bathe in
a million bottles of wine. The long-suffering official produced the wine,
Li bathed in it and was cured. He announced that the official and his
wife had successfully passed the test of worthiness, and told them and
the servants to bathe in wine. When they emerged, they found their
youth returned.

Li Po (699–762). Chinese poet. See *Eight Immortals of the Wine Cup*.

Li T'ieh-kuai The Fifth of the Eight Immortals (q.v.).

Liu An see *Huai Nan Tzu*.

Liu-hai Hsien He was a minister of state under the Kitan ruler Yeh-lü
Cho-li-chih, and retired to go into retreat on Mount T'ai Hua, in Hsi-an
[Xian].

One day, when a minister, he received a visitor, Han Chung-li, who
began to demonstrate a trick, balancing ten eggs on top of each other

with gold coins between. When Liu-hai expressed his anxiety at the danger of the trick, the Immortal replied that it was not as dangerous as his own position. He knew what the visitor meant, and subsequently resigned his post.

He travelled in search of perfection, meeting Lü Tung-pin of the Eight Immortals (q.v.) who gave him the recipes for turning gold into immortality pills.

He is said to have been accompanied by a three-legged toad, which often made its escape to the nearest well, whereupon Liu-hai had to lure it out using strings of gold coins as bait.

He is usually represented with the three-legged toad, the string of coins, and a belt of coins and eggs. He is sometimes invoked as a god of wealth, on account of his string of gold coins which he uses to tempt his three-legged toad, always shown close by. The picture is usually a double one, pasted on the two facing leaves of a door. He is also patron deity of needlemakers.

Liu Hsi, King of Lu-Chiang see *Huai Nan Tzu*.

Liu Ken A fang-shih (q.v.) mentioned in the History of the Later Han dynasty. He was summoned by the governor, Ch'i, for practising magic, and ordered to explain himself, under threat of execution. Liu Kan turned to the left and whistled, whereupon Ch'i's ancestral ghosts appeared. To the governor's shame, they publicly admonished Ch'i for neglecting his ancestral rites, then, along with Liu Ken, vanished.

Liu-meng Chiang-chün Guardian against grasshoppers and locusts. He is depicted as a beardless young man, fond of children. Several historic persons are said to be the original Liu-meng, as a result of which several spurious temples were closed down during the reign of Emperor K'ang Hsi (1662–1723). His day is the thirteenth of the first moon. (See also *Pa Cha*.)

Lohan Disciples of the Buddha, in non-Chinese terminology, Arhat (with various spellings). Arhat transmuted into Arhan, and from that into Lohan. The Arhat are the guardians of the scriptures, as expounded by Sakyamuni. Of the Eighteen Lohan usually shown on the walls of Buddhist temples and monasteries, sixteen are of Hindu origin, but the origin and identity of the remaining two are obscure. In addition to the Eighteen Lohan, there are many other disciples who have conquered all passion and attained Nirvana. For example, there are temples to the Five Hundred Lohan, one such celebrated temple being in Canton [Guang Dong], while some Buddhist sources give each of the five hundred lohan numerous bands of followers, all of whom are lohan.

Lohan, The Eighteen The Buddha (q.v.), having attained his eightieth year, entrusted the diffusion of religion to the god Indra, and four great Bikshu (followers or 'apostles') called (a) Maha Kasyapa (Kashiapa), in Chinese, Ma-ho Chia-yeh; (b) Pindola (Pin-tu-lo); (c) Kun Dadhana (Chün T'ou-p'o-han); and (d) Rahula (Lo-hu-lo).

From these four Bikshu followed the sixteen Arhat, revered in China, Japan and Korea, though not in India. Having probably originated in Kashmir, the sixteen Arhat were first mentioned in the Mahayana-vataraka, translated into Chinese in AD 437, but only Pindola and Rahula are mentioned by name. A full transcription of the sixteen names did not appear until given by Hsüan Tsang (q.v.) in 653. This leaves the seventeenth and eighteenth to be explained. In the Sung dynasty, there is a reference to the fact that there were sixteen Lohan, but that eighteen were sometimes mentioned. By the end of the tenth century, the number eighteen was firmly fixed in the public mind, the additional two being the Arhats who tamed the Dragon and the Tiger (Dragon and Tiger are symbolic of East and West respectively). They may have been an allegorical reference to the triumph of Buddhism over Taoism, since the Dragon and Tiger are Taoist symbols. In some portrayals of the Eighteen Lohan, the seventeenth place is allocated to Nandimitra, and the eighteenth is a repetition of the first, Pin-tu-lo Po-lo-to-she. Various names have been put forward for the seventeenth and eighteenth Lohan, but the real reason there are eighteen and not sixteen is that they followed an existing Chinese tradition. In AD 621 the Emperor T'ai Tsung set up a select college of eighteen learned scholars, who provided on a rota basis a select council of three to be permanently on duty to advise the Emperor on all matters.

But although the sixteen Lohan of Hsüan Tsang may be considered as the original list, with the two additions, there are other lists of Eighteen Lohan which differ considerably. The most important is the Eighteen Lohan of Wu-wei, and there are many others, notably the Eighteen Lohan of Tibet.

The Eighteen Lohan have distinguishing symbols, badges or poses, but there is considerable variation. The four Bikshu are sometimes shown with ear-rings, to signify their superior rank. Not surprisingly, some artists confuse the Eighteen Lohan with the Eight Immortals (q.v.), and depict them crossing the sea to the land of Nirvana, or dwelling in the K'un Lun paradise.

The original sixteen Arhat, with their Chinese and Sanskrit names, are:

1. *Pin-tu-lo Po-lo-to-she (Pindola the Bharadvaja)*; explained as Pu-tung: Not-moving; the second of the Bikshu. He lived in the land of Wheat, to the West. His voice was like the roar of a lion, and he was fond of exhibiting his magical powers, such as floating over the heads of a crowd in a wooden boat, for which he was rebuked by the Buddha.

   He is portrayed with very long eyebrows, with an alms-bowl, open book and pilgrim's staff. He is said to have lived on tiles and stones for nourishment, and hence is often portrayed thin and skeletal.

2. *Chia-no-chia Fa-ts'o (Kanaka-Vatsa)*. Heard the Law from Buddha's own lips. Could understand all expositions of the Law, no matter how abstruse. His Tibetan name means Golden Calf. He was appointed to teach in Kashmir, and may have been the source of the idea of the Sixteen (or Eighteen) Lohan.

3. *Chia-no-chia Po-li-to-she (Kanaka the Bharadvaja)*. Usually portrayed as being very hairy, accompanied by a young disciple.

4. *Su-p'in-t'e (Subhinda)*. Revered in temples throughout Japan, Korea and China. Portrayed as a sage with a scroll, alms bowl, incense vase, with a distinctive finger-clicking gesture. This symbolizes that he was enlightened in the time it takes to snap the fingers.

5. *No-ch'ü-lo (Nakula)*. As *nakula* translates as a bag made of mongoose skin, he is portrayed with either that creature or, in Tibet, with the three-legged toad from Chinese mythology.

6. *Po-t'o-lo (Bhadra)*. A cousin to the Buddha Sakyamuni, sometimes shown with a tiger companion.

7. *Chia-li-chia (Kalika)*. Another Lohan portrayed with long eyebrows, which he holds up from the ground, and sometimes holding a leaf.

8. *Fa-she-lo Fu-to-lo (Vajraputra)*; *Son of the Thunderbolt*. Portrayed very hairy and skeletal.

9. *Shu-po-chia (Supaka)*. Also known as Chieh-po-ka. An elder who taught near Patna. Portrayed with a holy man at his right shoulder, and holding a book or fan.

10. *Pan-t'o-chia (Panthaka)*. He and his twin brother (see 16, below) were born on the roadside while their mother was making a journey. Thus, being born on the way was symbolic of their propagating the truth. In addition to his gifts of teaching, he was

able to fly through walls, levitate, and conjure up fire and water. When necessary, he could reduce his size to a dot. He is usually depicted sitting under a tree with arms folded, and sometimes charming a dragon.

11. *Lo-hu-lo (Rahula); fourth of the Bikshu.* He lived in the Land of Millet. The eldest son of Sakyamuni (q.v.) the Buddha, and will be reincarnated as the eldest son of every future Buddha. Hsüan Tsang (q.v.) reported seeing his statue when he visited Kapilavastu. He is sometimes represented with a large head, bulging eyes and hooked nose, and is the patron of Buddhist novices.

12. *Chia-hsi-na (Nagasena).* Said to have been born in AD 43, he became a renowned authority of the Hinayana (Lesser Vehicle) doctrine.

13. *Yin-chieh-t'o (Angida).* Said to be an incarnation of Maitreya (Mi-lo Fo) (q.v.), and as such, represented as jolly and fat; otherwise he is shown as an ascetic, old and thin, leaning on a staff and holding a book with Indian characters.

14. *Fa-na-p'o-ssu (Vanavasa).* Heard the Law from Buddha's lips. Depicted meditating in a cave, making a magic gesture or nursing his right knee.

15. *A-shih-to (Asita).* The Invincible. Was formerly a Brahman rishi (sage) who became a follower of Buddha. He is shown as an old sage with long eyebrows, holding his right knee.

16. *Chu-ch'a Pan-t'o-chia (Chota Panthaka).* Twin brother of the tenth Lohan (above) and also invested with magical powers. He produced five hundred oxen out of nowhere and rode one through the air. Shown as an old man leaning on a dead tree, one hand holding a fan, the other raised, or sometimes holding a staff with a hare's head on top, or a broom under his gown.

Lohan of Wu Wei, The Eighteen The Wu-wei version of the Eighteen Lohan has only seven Hindu names, and introduces others of purely Chinese origin. The seventeenth and eighteenth may in fact be the Lohan who subdued the Dragon and Tiger, referred to above.

1. *Wu-k'o Ch'an-shih (The Rook's-Nest Zen Master).* He lived at the top of a tree, primarily to escape the cares and troubles of the world, but also because he foresaw, and wished to avoid, the Great Flood which occurred in the time of the Emperor Yao (2357–2255 BC). The suspicion is that this Buddhist tale must have been borrowed

from Taoist lore. He is portrayed sitting in the branches of a tree.

2. *Tzu-ts'ai Ch'an-shih (Isvara the Zen Master)*. Yüan dynasty; for quelling a rebellion by his magic powers, he was buried alive, and decapitated five times. Shown holding a fly-whisk.

3. *Tao-t'ung Ch'an-shih*. AD 733–813; born Anhui, died in Ssuch'uan (Szechwan). Companion of Feng-kan (next.) Shown sitting on a mat, hugging his knees.

4. *Feng-kan Ch'an-shih*. Eighth century. A giant, seven feet tall. Rode a tiger; (see Po-t'o-lo, No. 6, above); found Shih-teh, and took him to a monastery to be raised and educated. Shown riding the tiger.

5. *Hui-yüan Ch'an-shih*. Early fifth century. A renowned Taoist, converted to Buddhism after visions of Amitabha (O-mi-t'o).

6. *Shih-teh Tzu (The Foundling)*. Found by Feng-kan (No. 4, above), and raised at a monastery.

7. Han-shan Tzu (Cold Mountain Philosopher). Famous eighth-century hermit-poet. He lived off charity in a cold cave in Chiang-hsi (Kiangsi), writing poetry on rocks and walls. He was said to have been very ugly, wearing a tree-bark hat, and dressed in rags. Like Pan-t'o-chia (No. 10, above) he also had the power to reduce himself to microscopic size, in order to hide in the crevices of the rocks.

8. *Hui-tsang Ch'an-shih*. Seventh century; born in Anhui. Found a statue of Maitreya (Mi-lo Fo (q.v.)) and erected it in a temple. Portrayed standing, bare-chested, with a gold head-band.

9. *Chü-ti Ho-shang (Gonamati the Monk)*. One of the Buddha's chief disciples, called Teh-hui, Virtue and Wisdom, by the Chinese. Portrayed as an old man sitting at the foot of a tree, with his hand raised in a teaching gesture.

10. *Tao-yüeh Ch'an-shih (Way of the Moon Zen Master, the Golden Island Monk)*. He lived on Golden Island, Kiangsu. He was consulted by the General Fei (1103–41) as to the meaning of a dream in which two dogs pursued him, and forced him to cross a river. The monk told him that the elements of his dream formed the character for 'prison' which was a bad omen, and warned the General not to cross the river, or he would perish in the storm. The general did not believe him, and proceeded to cross the river safely. However, on arrival at his destination, he was arrested, thrown into prison, and executed.

Tao-yueh is shown seated, resting his head on his hand, and lost in meditation.

11. *Shih-Tzu-pi-ch'iu Tsun-che (Singhalaputra) Son of the Lion*. A Brahman from India who converted to the Contemplative (Ch'an) school. He taught that to do nothing, observe nothing, and adhere to nothing would bring Nirvana on earth. He was denounced by court officials he had offended, and executed. He is shown standing, with a pilgrim's staff, and attended by a disciple.

12. *Ts'ung-shen Ch'an-shih*. Ninth century, lived in Shantung. Founder of a school of meditation at Chao Chou, in Chihli. Shown standing, with a teaching gesture, holding a broom concealed by his sleeve.

13. *Lo-hou-lo-to Tsun-che (Rahulata)*. Attained Nirvana 113 BC. A renowned teacher and miracle worker, on one occasion producing rice from Heaven to feed the throng of people listening to him. Shown as an old man sitting on a rock, holding a pilgrim's staff.

14. *Shen-tsan Ch'an-shih or Lan Ts'an, the Lazy Glutton*. Lived in the reign of Hsüan Tsang, about AD 742. He was employed as a kitchen porter in a monastery, and gained a reputation for eating the leftovers of the monks' meals. He used to sleep in the cattle pen, but chanted his prayers at midnight, his resonant voice filling the valleys. He was visited by the scholar Li Pi, and told he would become Prime Minister and occupy the position for ten years, which proved to be true.

Apparently he had other powers. For example it took only a touch of his foot to move a heavy rock which ten oxen could not budge. When he left the monastery the valley became plagued with wild beasts which had never been there before. But he returned, jumped on the back of a tiger, and rode away. Neither he nor the wild beasts were seen again.

He is shown standing, holding a staff which he rests on the back of his neck, and with a hat over his shoulder.

15. *Chiu-mo-lo-to Tsun-che (Kumarajiva)*. AD 360–415. Renowned for his translations of the scriptures. Shown with a lion and a dove.

16. *Mo-ho Chia-yeh Tsun-che (Maha Kasyapa)*. The first of the four Bikshu (q.v.). A Brahman of Central India, one of the first disciples of the Buddha. When an earthquake occurred, Kasyapa divined the cause as the death of the Buddha, and immediately called for an assembly of five hundred Arhat in the cave of Sattapani at Gridkrakuta, and compiled the first Canon of Buddhism.

He is shown as an old man with long eyebrows; he holds a staff in one hand, and a scroll containing the Buddhist scriptures in the other.

17. *Ma-ming Tsun-che (Asvagosha)*. Born in the first century in Benares; died in Kashmir about AD 100. Ma-ming means 'neighing of a horse' and refers to an incident in the teacher's life. After Asvagosha had converted five hundred noble youths to Buddhism, the King of Scythia, Kanishka, was afraid that with so many converts to the monastic life, the population would be depleted. The king tried to disrupt the teacher's instruction by keeping seven horses without food, and then putting their fodder out where Asvagosha was preaching. The horses, however, shed tears on hearing the teacher's words, and listened attentively. Thus Asvagosha's voice was said to be like the neighing of a horse, since the animals could understand him.

He is shown sitting on a rock, his left shoulder bare, his left hand raised, contemplating a dragon.

18. *Pu-tai Ch'an-shih (Pu-tai Ho-shang) The Calico Bag Zen Master*. Buddhist Lohan and Taoist Immortal. Official name Chang Ting-tzu, died AD 917. He is said to be the last incarnation of Maitreya, or Mi-lo Fo (q.v.), hence the symbolism of the calico bag. He slept in the open, and by the type of shoes he wore, the local populace were able to foretell the weather. He is one of the privileged few to be invited to the banquet of Hsi Wang Mu (q.v.).

He is shown sitting, with the bag at his feet or hanging from a staff over his shoulder.

Lo-hou and Chi-tu (Rahu and Ketu) The Moon's nodes are the points where the Moon's path round the Earth crosses the Earth's path round the Sun. The point where the Moon crosses 'upwards' (i.e. northwards) is called the ascending node, or the Dragon's head, referred to by Indian astronomers as Rahu, and transliterated into Chinese as Lo-hou. The other node, always lying directly opposite the north node, is the Dragon's Tail, Ketu, or Chi-tu. In Chinese astrological lore, they are considered to be invisible planets, and as such they are regarded as the abodes of celestial beings.

Lo-hou, the Star of Quarrels, is the residence of P'eng Tsun, a general of Chou Wang (q.v.), while his companion in arms, Wang Pao, occupies Chi-tu.

Lo-hu-lo (Rahula) see *Lohan, The Eighteen*.

Longevity see *Elixir of Life; Fu Lu Shou.*

Longevity Star see *Old Man of the South Pole.*

Lo P'an A Chinese compass used by feng-shui (q.v.) practitioners. The term means net plate, on account of its plate-like shape, and its being engraved with numerous divisions, like a round net. They are of various sizes and degrees of complexity, but all are considered to be powerful talismans against evil spirits.

The various bands of divisions, from the centre outwards, refer to the Eight Diagrams (q.v.), the Lo Shu (q.v.), the points of the compass, the seasons of the year, and the twenty-eight lunar mansions (q.v.).

Lo Shen (Lu Shen). See *Fu Lu Shou.*

Lo Shu The Book of the (River) Lo. A mystic diagram revealed to Fu Hsi (q.v.). In fact, it is the mathematical 'magic square' arrangement of the numbers 1 to 9 so that they add up to 15 in each direction.

$$4 \quad 9 \quad 2$$
$$3 \quad 5 \quad 7$$
$$8 \quad 1 \quad 6$$

See also *Yü.*

Lost legends Despite the vast richness of legends and myths in Chinese literature and folklore, archaeological excavations often reveal tantalizing glimpses of legends that have been forgotten. The famous banner of Ma Wang Tui (q.v.), for example, shows two horse-riders suspending a bell, supporting another vessel containing something which attracts birds. There is no known Chinese legend which incorporates these elements. But the most outstanding omission is the well-known image of the Hare in the Moon, pounding away at herbs in a vat to make the elixir of life. As familiar as the picture is, there is nothing in early Chinese literature to suggest how the Hare got to the Moon, or why. Other remarkable pointers to lost traditions are the ceremonial artefacts, the *tsung* and *pi*, usually made of jade, which have an important ritual significance. The *tsung* is a vase-like cylinder, and the *pi* a disc. They are obviously modelled on some useful object, like the ju-i sceptre (q.v.), but their original purpose has not been discovered.

Lo-tsu Ta Hsien A disciple of Lao Tzu (q.v.) who gave up the religious life and became a street barber. Patron of barbers and corn-cutters.

Lo Yü Patron of tea (q.v.).

Luan see *Phoenix*.

Lu-chiang, King of, see *Huai Nan Tzu*.

Lu-hu-lo see *Lohan, The Eighteen*.

Lunar mansions see *Mansions, Lunar; Zodiac*.

Lung Wang Dragon King; either a king who is a dragon, or the king of the dragons, or a water-monster generally. For dragons generally, see *Dragons*.

In Chinese mythology, the principal dragon king, or King of the Dragons, is Ao Kuang, followed by his son, Ao Ping. Fighting on the side of Chou Wang (q.v.), Ao Ping was killed by Li No-cha (q.v.).

Another notable dragon king is the White Dragon, Pai Lung, whose history is preserved on a stone tablet at the White Dragon Temple on Mount Yang, Suchow, Kiangsu. During the time of Emperor An (AD 379–419) a young girl met an old man, who begged her to shelter him from the coming storm. The next morning she was found to be with child, and her parents expelled her from their home. In the course of time, she gave birth to a lump of flesh, which she threw into the water. It then turned into a white dragon, and approached her, but she fell into a faint. A terrible storm came up, and the dragon took flight, leaving the girl in a swoon from which she never recovered. The locals buried her, and her tomb became a popular shrine to the Mother of the White Dragon.

Chang-lung, a magistrate during the reign of Chung Tsung (AD 684), had a fine wife, a respected post, and nine sons. However, one day, after a fishing trip, he took to the strange practice of spending the night in a temple, then returning home every morning wet and cold. He explained that he was now a dragon, but that he had been ejected from the temple by another dragon, whom he must fight for supremacy. He told his nine sons that they would be able to recognize him in the ensuing contest by the fact that he would be wearing a red ribbon. The sons dutifully shot the rival dragon, who left the neighbourhood and expired.

The temple where the dragon took residence, became the focal point for worship of Chang-lung from AD 707, and a larger temple was built in 894. In 1091, a year of great drought, special prayers were offered to Chang-lung to bring rain, and when the petition succeeded, the people gratefully enlarged his temple.

The Golden Dragon, so called, is not really a dragon at all, but simply got the name from the place where he was born. Hsieh Hsü was the nephew of Empress Hsieh (1225-65); being the fourth son, he was known as Number Four. In 1265 the Mongols attacked and abducted the Empress and her heir apparent. To avoid capture and humiliation, the nephew first disguised himself as a Buddhist monk, then drowned himself. Before committing himself to the water, he made certain prophecies relating to the vengeance that would come. The people collected his body, and buried it at the Golden Dragon Mountain. A century later, the spirit of Hsieh Hsü came to the aid of Hung Wu (1368-99), the founder of the Ming dynasty, and helped him to overthrow the Mongols by plaguing them with bees. He was subsequently called Chin-lung Ssu Ta Wang, Golden Dragon Number Four Great King.

The term dragon king is also used for *naga*, or serpent king, in Chinese translations of Buddhist and Hindu literature. (See also *Hsüan Tsang*.)

Lu Pan [Lu Ban] The patron deity of carpenters and builders, commemorated on the twelfth day of the sixth lunar month.

Lu Pan is the familiar name given to the historical figure, Kung-shu Tze, born 506 BC, referred to in the works of Mencius. He is the hero of many folk-tales, some of which attest to his supernatural powers. For example, when his father was falsely accused of a crime, and executed by the governors of the state of Wu, Lu Pan carved a statue whose outstretched arm pointed accusingly at Wu. The city fell under a prolonged drought, until eventually, near starvation, the people repented and appealed to Lu Pan to lift the curse. Touched by their remorse, he cut off the hand of the statue, whereupon rain fell immediately.

Most stories of Lu Pan, however, underline his marvellous skills as a mechanic, ascribing to him the invention of such everyday utilities as the carpenter's horse, ball and socket joints, and so forth. Usually, Lu Pan is depicted as a wandering artisan, travelling incognito, mysteriously appearing when most needed to give inspired advice to master builders faced with apparently insurmountable problems.

He was awarded the title Grand Master, Sustainer of the Empire, by the Yung Lo Emperor (1403-25). (See also *Tsui-erh*.)

Lü-shih A member of an order of ascetic Buddhists, as distinct from the contemplative (*ch'an-shih*, q.v.) or teaching (*fa-shih*, q.v.) orders.

Lu Su First century. He was imprisoned for a political crime, but earned the respect of the prison governor because of his anxiety for his mother's welfare. As a consequence, the governor released him. One of the Twenty-Four Examples of Filial Piety (q.v.).

Lü Tung-pin The Third of the Eight Immortals (q.v.).

M

Mencius

Maitreya see *Mi-lo Fo*.

Ma Ku The Hemp Lady. The popular name given to three different women who attained immortality.

1. A famous female magician who lived in the time of the Later Han dynasty, during the reign of Emperor Huan Ti (AD 147–68), at Tan-ch'eng in Shantung. She reclaimed a large tract of land from the sea, and planted it with mulberry trees.

    An image of her is presented to married couples on their silver and golden wedding anniversaries.

2. A reincarnation of the first Ma Ku, living during the reign of Chao Wang (AD 328–32). Her father, Ma Hu, was so cruel that mothers used his name to threaten their children when they misbehaved or cried. His slaves were only allowed to stop work when the cock crew, so she imitated the cockcrow an hour earlier to give them more rest. Her father was so violently angry that she ran away and became a hermit. When she had gone, however, the father was

overcome with remorse, and went blind through weeping. Hearing of his plight, the daughter returned, and bathed his eyes with some special wine that she had made. In spite of his pleas, she did not stay, but left on the back of a bird.

3. Lived c. 1111; born in Kiangsi, and became a hermit on Ma-yü Mountain, Shantung. The Emperor awarded her the title Chen Jen in recognition of her goodness.

Ma Mien The Horse-faced Messenger from Hell (q.v.), together with Ox-head, Niu T'ou, they attend on Yen Lo as assistants to the Wu-ch'ang Kuei (q.v.). Their images are also placed in the temple of the City God, Ch'eng Huang (q.v.).

Mang Shen see Ox, The Spring.

Mansions, Lunar The twenty-eight lunar mansions are constellations which lie along the celestial equator, similar to the constellations of the Western zodiac (q.v.). Each of them is the abode of a spirit which rules each day in turn, the first, eighth, fifteenth and twenty-second mansions always occurring on a Sunday. Two of the constellations, the Ox and the Maiden, which lie either side of the Milky Way, are associated with the popular legend of the Ox-Boy and the Weaving Maid (q.v.). The constellations form four groups of seven, each group being associated with one of the seasons and its celestial emblem (q.v.).

Taoist authorities offer different names for the names of the spirits. One source says that they were all disciples of the Taoist T'ung-t'ien Chiao-chu who achieved immortality. In another, they were all animals, later transmigrated into human beings, and later became Immortals. But in the Battle of the Ten Thousand Spirits (q.v.) they took the side of Chou Wang, and being slain, took up their abodes in the twenty-eight mansions.

The following table gives the names of the twenty-eight mansions, the animal attendant, the names of the attendant spirits, and the disciples of T'ung-t'ien Chiao-chu. The animals marked with an asterisk are those which popularly replace the twelve branches (q.v.).

Stars and Spirits of the Green Dragon of Spring and the East

1. The Dragon's Horn	*Scaly Dragon	Teng Yu	Po-lin Tao-jen
2. The Dragon's Neck	Smooth Dragon	Wu Han	Li-Tao-t'ung
3. The Base of the House	Badger	Chia Fu	Kao-p'ing Tao-jen
4. The Room	*Rabbit	Keng Yen	Yao Kung-po
5. The Dragon's Heart	Fox	K'ou Hsin	Su-yüan Tao-jen
6. The Dragon's Tail	*Tiger	Ts'en P'eng	Chu Chao
7. The Basket	Leopard	Feng I	Yang Chen

Stars and Spirits of the Black Tortoise of Winter and the North

8.	The Ladle	Unicorn	Chu Yu	Yang Hsin
9.	The Ox	•Ox	Chi Tsun	Li Hung
10.	The Maiden	Bat	Ching Tan	Cheng-yüan Tao-jen
11.	Void	•Rat	Kai Yen	Chou Pao
12.	The Rooftop	Swallow	Chien Tan	Hou T'ai-i
13.	The House	•Pig	Keng Shun	Kao Chen
14.	The Wall	Porcupine	Tsang Kuan	Fang Chi-ch'ing

Stars and Spirits of the White Tiger of Autumn and the West

15.	The Slipper	Wolf	Ma Wu	Li Hsiung
16.	The Mound	•Dog	Liu Lung	Chang-hsiung Tao-jen
17.	The Stomach	Pheasant	Wu Ch'eng	Sung Ken
18.	Pleiades	•Cock	Wang Liang	Huang Ts'ang
19.	The Net	Crow	Ch'en Chün	Chin Shen-yang
20.	The Beak	•Monkey	Fu Chün	Fang Kuei
21.	Orion	Ape	Tu Mao	Sun Hsiang

Stars and Spirits of the Red Bird of Summer and the South

22.	The Well	Wild Dog	Yao Ch'i	Shen Keng
23.	The Ghost	•Sheep	Wang Pa	Chao Pai-kao
24.	The Willow	Buck	Jen Kuang	Wu K'un
25.	The Bird Star	•Horse	Li Chung	Lü Neng
26.	The Bow	Deer	Wan Hsiu	Hsieh Ting
27.	The Wing	•Snake	P'ei T'ung	Wang Chiao
28.	The Carriage	Worm	Liu Chih	Hu Tao-yüan

Ma-t'ou Niang The Horse Head Lady. See *Ts'an Nü*.

Ma Wang King of the Horses. (Not to be confused with Mu Wang, famed for his Eight Horses.) According to the Book of Rites of the Chou dynasty, Ma Wang is the name of the celestial horse for the star Fang, the fourth of the twenty-eight lunar mansions (q.v.). Ma Wang is represented as a three-faced god showing the faces of Ma Tsu, the ancestor of horses, Hsien Mu, the first breeder of horses, and Ma She, the first riding-master.

Paper prints are burnt in his honour which portray him as a king accompanied by his officers. He is then named Ssu-ma Ta Shen, the Great Spiritual Cavalier. In other portrayals he is shown accompanied by a dragon, a phoenix and a crane.

Ma Wang Tui One of the most important archaeological sites in China, discovered in 1972 in Hu-nan. The tomb, dating from 202 BC, supplied many valuable paintings and other tangible descriptions of early Chinese mythology, and pre-date the writings of Huai Nan Tzu (q.v.) and Ssu-ma Ch'ien (q.v.) by a lifetime.

In establishing what are the oldest and original features of Chinese legends the Banner of Ma Wang Tui is a valuable witness. The Toad (q.v.), the Hare (q.v.) and the Crow (q.v.) are all shown with Hsi Wang Mu, revealing that these essential ingredients featured in the earliest legends. The following details reveal what aspects of mythology were current at the time the painting was made.

Firstly, there are the Isles of P'eng-lai, the home of various spiritual creatures who distilled the elixir of immortality. As the islands lacked any solid foundations, however, and were in danger of floating away, it was necessary for them to be anchored by giant turtles, two of which are shown in the painting. Another legend says that one of the inhabitants of the isles is Yü Ch'iang, who has a human face and a bird's body, and that serpents hang from his ears, and the banner shows a figure which could represent Yü Ch'iang, although in place of serpents the painting shows ribbons.

That Heaven had a gate, guarded by two gatekeepers is also evident from the painting, which depicts them as a tiger and a leopard. Also shown is the Fu-sang tree, which gave shelter to the Ten Suns (q.v.). Two dragons are depicted, one with wings, the other without, the former to draw the moon and the other the sun through the sky. The winged dragon assisted Yü the Great by drawing lines on the earth to show where the water-course should run.

See also *Lost Legends*.

Mencius Meng K'o, or Meng Tzu, 372–289 BC, philosopher. His writings form the fourth of the Four Books, one of the great exponents of the teachings of Confucius (q.v.).

Meng Ch'ang see *Chang Hsien*.

Meng Tsung Third century. His mother having sent him out in winter for bamboo shoots, he roamed the forests despairing of finding them out of season. Suddenly, as a reward for his devotion, they began to sprout through the ground. One of the Twenty-Four Examples of Filial Piety (q.v.).

Metal See *Elements, the Five*.

Mid-autumn Festival The 15th day of the Eighth Moon, the eighth month being the one in which the autumn equinox occurs, and the fifteenth day being when the moon is full. At that time, for meteorological reasons, the full moon (the 'harvest moon' to Westerners) always appears much bigger than usual. It was customary to have Moon-Watching parties, and offerings are still made to the

Moon. It is a time for great celebration, with special foods, including the celebrated Moon Cakes, and paper lanterns are in abundance.

The autumn equinox marks the time of the year when nights become longer than the days, and as the Moon symbolizes the Yin, or feminine force, the rituals are performed by women, who offer incense and food at altars in the open air. In cities, the ceremonies are held in private, but in country districts there is ritual dancing and spiritualist seances. (See also *Ch'ang O.*)

Mi-lo Fo (Maitreya) Mi-lo the Buddhist; also Hsiao Fo, the Laughing Buddha. Elected by Sakyamuni (q.v.) to be his successor after five thousand years, when the world would have become so corrupt that the Law would have been forgotten. In that sense, he is the Buddhist equivalent of the Messiah.

He is represented as fat and squat, with the left leg crosswise in front of the body, and long ear-lobes which reach the shoulders, and usually with long flowing locks. He is shown with his torso bare, and he has a laughing expression. There is usually a rosary in his right hand, every bead of which represents a hundred years, while in his left he carries a bag containing *chi-mu*, the mother breath or primordial matter.

Maitreya, as patron of goldsmiths and silversmiths, is the Buddhist equivalent to Tung-fang Shuo (q.v.).

Mi-lo, on leaving the palace of Shih-chia (Sakyamuni), appropriated some gold and silver ingots which he worked on and made into jewellery in order to earn a living.

He was apprehended by Lü Tung-pin (q.v.), and tied up with a magic chain. This chain is the origin of the *pai-so sheng*, the plaited cord placed around the necks or wrists of young children and others to bind them to Buddha.

Min Sun (551–479 BC) A disciple of Confucius (q.v.). While his father was away, his stepmother, having two children of her own, treated him badly and only gave him leaves to wear. When the father returned, he was so angry at the stepmother's treatment of his son that he wanted to send her away, but Min Sun interceded for her, saying it was better that he should go cold, than that three children should be motherless. From then on, the grateful stepmother treated him affectionately. One of the Twenty-Four Examples of Filial Piety (q.v.).

Monkey Ninth of the twelve animals (q.v.) of the Chinese zodiac (q.v.).

Monkey King Sun Hou-tzu; the central character in the popular

Chinese romance, Journey to the West (q.v.), usually, but wrongly, attributed to Ch'iu Ch'ang-ch'un (1148–1227). The story is an allegory, Sun Hou-tzu representing human failings which can be redeemed, Chu Pa-chiai (the Pig) the baser nature which can be suppressed. The Priest Sha (q.v.) (sometimes translated as Friar Sand) represents human frailty, which is weak and in constant need of encouragement, and Hsüan Tsang the finer nature, which can attain immortality. Similarly, Sun Hou-tzu's iron rod symbolizes the power of the doctrine.

Although the work has been a favourite piece of romantic fiction for several hundred years, it contains some interesting elements which are not generally appreciated. Throughout the work, there is a constant battle between the band of pilgrims and other powerful forces. Although right eventually prevails, right being, in this instance, the Buddhist Doctrine, the forces of Taoism are always shown to be powerful, and despite the miraculous attributes of the Monkey King, which saw him in equal combat with all the forces of Heaven, even he cannot overcome the magical forces of Taoism, and on a number of occasions the Buddha has to intervene. The message, enigmatically, is that while Buddhism is the superior religion, Taoism is equal to it.

Although perhaps ultimately of serious intent, the adventures were meant to entertain, and in this they succeeded; for not only is there both movement, action and suspense, there is humour too, as can be seen in the incidents at the Motherhood River, or in the land without monks.

Some of the main events of the narrative are reviewed elsewhere in this guide, listed under the name of the chief character appearing in the episode. Other highlights of the tale are outlined here. The numbers in brackets refer to the thirty-four books available in translation which comprise the Journey to the West.

(1) Sun Hou-tzu was born after a magic stone on the Hua Kuo Shan, the Mountain of Flowers and Fruit, ripened and split open. The Jade Emperor (q.v.) declared that Sun would be a fit companion for all the animal inhabitants of the mountain, and made him King of the Monkeys. He then travelled in search of knowledge, but on his return, found that his fellow monkeys had been troubled by an evil spirit, which he disposed of. Then he approached Ao Kuang, the Dragon King, for a magic weapon. Unfortunately, he did not use his powers well, and was summonsed to appear before Yü Huang (q.v.), the Jade Emperor.

(2) To keep him occupied, he was made Chief Groom of the Celestial Stables, but he considered this past far too inferior, and returned to

the Mountain of Flowers and Fruit. There he laid siege to the armies of Heaven, and declared himself to be Great Sage equal to Heaven. To appease him, the Jade Emperor appointed him guardian of the celestial peaches. Angry at not being invited to the Banquet of Peaches given by Hsi Wang Mu (q.v.), Monkey ate the peaches and while the guests were asleep, ate and drank all the food laid out at the banquet.

His mischief earned him the enmity of all the gods of Heaven. There were numerous attempts to catch him, most of which he evaded, until at last a magic ring was thrown at him. As it encircled his head, the Celestial Dog, T'ien Kou, bit him and held him until he was overpowered.

(3) He was sentenced to death, but having been endowed with immortality he could not be executed. Finally the Buddha asked him what he wanted most, which was to be supreme ruler of the universe. The Buddha agreed he would surrender his position to the Monkey provided that the Monkey could prove his superiority by leaping beyond his reach. The Monkey soared into space, right to the very edge of the cosmos, and as a sure sign that he had succeeded, signed his name on the boundary of the universe. He returned triumphant, but the Buddha merely showed him his hand, on which the Monkey had signed his name.

(4) Subdued at last, Monkey agreed to act as guide to Hsüan Tsang during his perilous mission to bring the scriptures back to China. The Emperor gave Hsüan Tsang a White Horse (q.v.), and the two set off on their journey. During the subsequent adventures, Hsüan Tsang lost his robe to the Black Bear Spirit, but managed to retrieve it through the Monkey's help. (5) Then they encountered a monster, the Pig Chu Pa-chiai, who reformed and joined the quest. (6) Their next obstruction was the giant, Sha, but he also reformed his ways to become a valued member of the band of adventurers.

(7) The journey was far from smooth; Monkey and Pig having robbed a temple garden, Hsüan Tsang was held as hostage and had to be rescued by his erring companions. (8) There was a delay when Monkey was sent back to the Fruit and Flowers Mountain, and Hsüan Tsang was captured by the White Bone Lady. (9) After Monkey had returned and rescued them, he had also had to effect their release from two demons, which he did by stealing their treasures, originally the property of Lao Tzu (q.v.).

(10) Their help is sought by others, too. The king of Wu Chi, who had been murdered for his throne by a lion, is restored to life and to his kingdom by the pilgrims. (11) For once, however, the Monkey had met his match in the Red Boy demon, and needed the assistance of a more powerful authority, Kuan Yin (q.v.), to save Hsüan Tsang.

Although the tales are about the bringing of the Buddhist scriptures to China, their author was a Taoist, so it is not unexpected to find figures from Buddhist history enlisting the aid of Taoist immortals. The next episode seems to serve the purpose of reconciling the two religions. (12) The companions reached a far-off kingdom where the Buddhist monks were forced to do the bidding of the Taoist priests, but after the Monkey defeated three demons, the king awarded the two religions equal status.

In the next sequence of events, the pilgrims defeated (13) a monster which was turned into a carp, (14) and another which turned out to be the fabulous Ox on which the philosopher Lao Tzu (q.v.) customarily travelled. (15) The next episode may have been the most unnerving experience of all; as a result of drinking from the Motherhood River, they all found themselves pregnant, which meant they had to drink from the Well of Miscarriage to resume their former condition.

(16) The party went from one feminizing adventure to another, for their next ordeal was to pass through the Land of Women, not the least of their difficulties being that the Queen of that country took a fancy to the monk Hsüan Tsang.

(17) Like many of the episodes, the next encounter Monkey has to face can be interpreted psychologically. He meets his reflection, equal to him in every way, both physically and in ingenuity. Only the Buddha is able to determine which is the imposter. (18) After the companions, using a magic plantain leaf to cool the fiery rocks, had crossed over a dangerous volcano, (19) they were accused of stealing treasure from the Golden Light Monastery. However, Monkey discovered that the treasure had been stolen by a nine-headed monster, and recovered it. (20) Reaching Little Thunder Mountain, it almost seemed that the party were to be defeated when all four of them were captured by a false Buddha, but the Jade Emperor sent the spirits of the twenty-eight lunar mansions (q.v.) to rescue them.

(21) They had to contend with natural hazards again when they crossed the Persimmon Mountain, because the rotting fruit made progress almost impossible. However, the Pig, with his omniverous snout, was able to clear a way through, and they progressed onwards (22) to find medicine for the ailing King of the Purple Country, rescue his queen, and retrieve his treasure which had been stolen.

(23) Although he resisted the advances of the Queen of the Land of Women, Hsüan Tsang was lured into a trap by the Seven Spider Women. When Monkey came to the Monk's aid, the Spider Women enlisted the help of a Taoist magician. His magic seemed to be too powerful for them until the Old Lady of Li advised Monkey to seek

the help of a Hindu deity, who rescued Hsüan Tsang and his companions. (24) The Buddha himself had to come to Hsüan Tsang's rescue yet again when he was kidnapped by demons posing as sedan-chair bearers. (25) Continuing their journey, the companions came to a country where the King was bewitched, and about to eat the hearts of 1,111 boy children. Fortunately, Monkey battled with the demon which caused the spell, who resumed his form as a white deer.

(26) Being the only mortal in the party, Hsüan Tsang could not see through the disguise of a mortal when he rescued a young woman, who was actually an evil spirit. Although she was unable to deceive Monkey, it was too late to save the monk, who was snatched away into a fathomless cavern. This time Monkey enlisted the help of King Li of the Cloud Tower Palace, whose officers managed to rescue the monk.

(27) When the party met their next obstacle, however, the Monkey was able to use the witty ingenuity for which he is famed. The country the companions had to pass through was ruled by a king who hated monks, and had them killed on sight. In the night, aided by his magical assistants, the Monkey shaved the heads of the entire court while they were asleep, so that they all looked like monks.

(28) The Monkey King had to use his powers of transformation to turn into a firefly to rescue the Monk, Pigsy and Friar Sand when they were lured into the lair of the Leopard Spirit, (29) but it was his powers of eloquence that brought help to a land smitten by drought. His coaxing words persuaded the ruler of the country to mend his ways, and Heaven rewarded the people with rain.

(30) Supernatural combat loomed again when the company reached the city of Yuhua, where they contended with the Yellow Lion demon, (31) and again on Green Dragon Mountain, where three rhinoceroses were posing as Buddhas.

(32) Hsüan Tsang and his companions finally reached India, but the monk's troubles were not yet over. A princess was about to choose a husband from her suitors by throwing a coloured ball into the air, and it landed on Hsüan Tsang. The Monkey, however, discerning that the princess was really an imposter, the Jade Hare, rescued the true princess, and the adventurers were able to set off once more on the last stages of their journey.

(33) Now close to their goal, they were met and entertained by a wealthy man, but shortly afterwards he was murdered and robbed. Hsüan Tsang and his companions were accused of the crime, but the Monkey King perceived that it was a plot contrived by the rich man's wife. To her consternation, the Monkey King raised her husband from the dead, and the conspiracy was revealed.

(34) Having spent fourteen years crossing nine kingdoms, and

covering ten thousand *li*, the pilgrims finally reached their destination and obtained the sacred scriptures. They returned to Ch'ang An, the capital of China, with 5,048 volumes which they presented to the T'ang Emperor T'ai Tsung. On his orders the doctrines were copied and distributed throughout the Empire.

See also *Hsüan Tsang; Sha Ho-shang; Chu Pa-chiai; White Horse.*

Mu, Battle of The epic Battle of Mu, in 1122 BC, between Chou Wang, the last ruler of the Yin (the latter part of the Shang) dynasty, and Wu Wang, the first ruler of the Chou dynasty, is the vehicle for a vast number of Chinese myths and legends. The historical events were recorded by Ssu-ma Ch'ien (q.v.) in the Shi Chi (Historical Records) but what is surprising is that although he wrote his account a thousand years after the battle, the details were substantiated by the discovery of inscriptions on commemorative bronze vessels cast at the time. However, according to legend, the terrestrial or mortal battle was paralleled by another battle of gods, spirits and immortals. The events of this celestial battle are recorded in the Book on the Making of Immortals, and the Catalogue of Spirits and Immortals, both of which are Taoist books compiled several centuries after the historical event. Many gods and spirits were annihilated in this battle, and several stellar dignitaries were replaced by newcomers to the celestial domains. It would be wrong, however, to suppose that the Battle of the Ten Thousand Spirits was a kind of Chinese *Götterdämmerung*, allegorizing the fall of one religion and its substitution by a new one, as many of the spiritual beings who took part in the Battle of the Ten Thousand Spirits were unknown, in chronological terms, at the time of the Battle of Mu. The following resumé outlines some episodes in the spiritual battle not dealt with elsewhere in this guide.

Li No-cha (q.v.) overcame the soldier-immortal Feng-lin (q.v.) by means of a Heaven–Earth bracelet. The soldier called on his superior, Chang Kuei-fang (q.v.), to assist him, but Li No-cha mounted his Wind–Fire wheel, on which he could travel about at rapid speed. Although Li No-cha heard his name called out three times, he continued to fight, and eventually broke Chang Kuei-fang's arm with his Heaven–Earth bracelet.

Li No-cha returned triumphantly to Chiang Tzu-ya, but was asked whether he had heard his name called during the battle. When Li No-cha said that he had, the general's face fell, for when Chang Kuei-fang calls a name, the human spirit (q.v.) separates, and the *hun* and *p'o* divide. Li No-cha, however, assured the general that he had changed himself into a lotus, which has neither *hun* nor *p'o* and therefore could not be harmed.

Chiang Tzu-ya decided to consult Wu Wang, and told the King he wanted to travel to the K'un Lun (q.v.) Mountain. The King warned him of the dangers involved, not so much to himself personally, but to the state if he left it at such a critical time. Chiang Tzu-ya, however, said that he would be gone for no more than three days.

On arriving at K'un Lun, he made his way to the Jade Palace, and was presented to Yüan-shih (q.v.). The Old Man of the South Pole (q.v.) gave him a list of Promotions to Immortality, and was told to erect a Spirit Terrace to display the list of honoured names. As Yüan-shih had warned him that on his return journey he must not pay attention to anyone calling his name, he resolutely pressed forward whenever this happened, but on the fourth occasion, the voice chided him, saying that because he was now a prime minister he no longer gave any thought to his friends of earlier years. He turned to the speaker, and saw it was a former colleague, Shen Kung-pao. But the newcomer wanted Chiang Tzu-ya to give up his loyalty to Wu Wang, and join Chou Wang's forces. What was even more sinister, was that Shen Kung-pao also tried to coax Chiang Tzu-ya into giving up the list of Promotions to Immortality. When Chiang Tzu-ya resisted, Shen Kung-pao offered to wager his magical skills against those of Chiang Tzu-ya, telling the general that he could take off his head and cause it to float through space. As this seemed to be unlikely, Chiang Tzu-ya accepted the challenge, promising to burn the list of Promotions to Immortality if Shen Kung-pao succeeded. At that, Shen Kung-pao took his sword and cut off his own head, and threw it into the air. Fortunately, the Old Man of the South Pole had been keeping a careful watch, and seeing that Chiang Tzu-ya was about to lose the vital document, sent the White Crane Youth, Pai-ho T'ung-tzu (q.v.) to carry off the head. But Chiang Tzu-ya, knowing he had lost the wager, felt honour-bound to keep his word to Shen Kung-pao, and asked the Old Man of the South Pole to return the head. This the old man did with reluctance, but then berated the reconstituted Shen Kung-pao so soundly that the culprit was thoroughly ashamed, and rode off angrily on his tiger.

After the K'eng San Ku-niang sisters (q.v.) had been thwarted by Lao Tzu (q.v.), the Old Man of the South Pole challenged Chang Shao, who tried to destroy him with hot sand. The venerable immortal easily encountered the attack with his seven-feathered fan, and was unharmed, while the attacker was swiftly dispatched by the White Crane Youth's jade sceptre.

Meanwhile, Wu Wang had been killed by Wen Chung (q.v.), but Jan-teng Tao-jen (q.v.) having first obliged Wen Chung, as a victor's duty, to wash the corpse and prepare it for burial, was able to revive the king with an elixir which he had with him.

It was now time for Wu Wang's forces to reassemble and resume the attack on Wen Chung. Hearing the forces approaching, Wen Chung mounted his black unicorn and galloped into the fracas. After numerous skirmishes, Wu Wang's armies marched forward, and Wen Chung was eventually forced to retreat. (See also *Ch'iung Hsiao; Heng Ha Erh Chiang; Kao, The Two Brothers; K'eng San Ku-niang; Lei Tsu.*)

Mu Kung see *Elements, The Five (Wood).*

Mu-jen *Mu-jen* [*mu-ren*], meaning wooden man, may be realistically translated as voodoo or witchcraft, since these words are popularly applied to the practice of making a figure of an enemy, and then subjecting it to various indignities in the belief that these will cause the victim to be struck by sympathetic injuries.

If made of wood, as the name implies, they are more effectively made from tung wood, or paulownia. There are two possible procedures: in the first, the effigy is meant to represent the victim, and after various sacrificial offerings have been made, it is buried; alternatively, a powerful spirit is invoked to possess the *mu-jen*, which is given a sword or other weapon to harm the victim. In the latter case, the effigy may be of paper, which is thrown at the accursed person.

There is yet another curious form of *mu-jen* used by *tao-nü*, or Tao-women, that is, taoist mediums who are not properly part of the established religion. They carry a carved wooden figure, about the size of the hand, which by manipulation and ventriloquism they appear to imbue with movement and speech. When one of the *tao-nü's* clients wishes to contact a departed relative, the *tao-nü* uses the *mu-jen* as a medium. She puts the *mu-jen* in her bosom, and after the spirit of the departed person has entered the *mu-jen*, it voices its reply. Alternatively, if the *tao-nü* has been called to attend to a sick person, the *mu-jen* may be filled with one of the spirits of epidemics, and declare the nature of the medicine to be taken.

An example of *mu-jen* was recorded in the semi-legendary history of the Battle of Mu (q.v.), but a more reliable historic incident is recorded as having occurred during the reign of the Han Emperor Wu Ti (q.v.).

The Emperor's favourite military commander, and his personal guard, was one Chiang-ch'ung (q.v.). When the Emperor woke in feverish fear from a nightmare, Chiang-ch'ung persuaded him that he was the victim of sorcery. Accordingly, the Emperor directed Chiang-ch'ung to find the perpetrators of his unease. The general employed a sorceress called Hu (like him, not ethnic Chinese but a Hun) as a witch-finder, and between them they claimed to have found a number of the wooden figures, *mu-jen*, bearing the names of the people who were supposed to have made them. Suspects were tortured to force them to reveal the names of their collaborators, until the number of the accused ran into thousands. He then proceeded against the Empress and the true heir to the throne, Li, digging up the floors of their apartments and demolishing the Empress's quarters so completely that it was said it was impossible to set up a bed for the night. More of the *mu-jen* were said to have been found, and Prince Li, being unable to convince his father of his innocence, fled to Honan, and there hanged himself.

Mu Wang, Emperor Fifth ruler of the Chou dynasty, 1001–746 BC. He was renowned for his Eight Horses (q.v.) who with their master-of-horse Tsao Fu, accompanied Mu Wang on his travels, even to his audience with Hsi Wang Mu (q.v.) at the Lake of Jewels.

N

Niu T'ou

Na-ka-hsi-na see Na-chia *Lohan, The Eighteen.*

Nan Chi Hsien-weng see *Old Man of the South Pole.*

New Year Customs The New Year is the main festival in the Chinese calendar. It occurs on the second full moon after the winter solstice, although there are many other attendant festivals both before and after New Year's Day. Fortune-tellers have a busy time, and the temples are thronged with people praying for success in the coming year, and seeking advice on love, health and business.

Preparation for the New Year begins on the twentieth of the last month, known as 'floor sweeping day'. Once all the detritus of the old year has been cleared out, a fresh start can be made. The Kitchen God, Tsao Chün (q.v.), makes his departure on the 23rd or 24th, and his paper image burned outside by the head of the family. As the New Year approaches, presents are exchanged, and on the 26th the Flower Fairs begin. It is also a time for settling all business transactions. Debts have to be paid off, but fortunately it is customary for employers to give an extra month's salary at the end of the year. Those debtors who could escape their creditors at the New Year were traditionally beyond the reach of settlement later.

It is traditional on New Year's Eve to paste verses on strips of red paper over the door and lintel. All food has to be prepared in advance, as it is unlucky to use scissors or knives on New Year's Day. A good joint of roast pork may well be served, while carp (q.v.), symbolic of long life, is an even more expensive delicacy associated with this time of year. Many foods are selected because their name is homonymous with some auspicious phrase (see *Rebus*), lettuce and cabbage, for example, sounding like the words for fortune and riches in Chinese.

Children are encouraged to stay up late and see the New Year in, and before midnight the doors are locked and sealed. At dawn they are opened, and incense offered to heaven and earth.

The following day is a special day of family reunions, and red packets containing money are given to younger relatives. Fire-crackers are lit to ward off evil spirits, and green branches are burnt to signify the passing of the old year.

Strictly speaking, New Year's Day should be a day of abstinence from meat, but it is usually regarded as sufficient for the first meal of the day to be a vegetarian one. The housewife may rest now, because no housework, particularly sweeping, should be done for two days, in case all the good luck is swept away. Children may be glad that they must not wash, either, but they must also be very careful not to fall or break anything, as that would be a bad omen.

On the second day, which is still a holiday, there is a round of visiting and entertainments, with gambling being particularly prominent, as everyone is sure that they are in for a lucky year. On the third day it is important to avoid quarrels, and it is also the traditional day for consulting the Chim (q.v.), or oracle. The next day the Kitchen God is welcomed back, and a new picture pasted up, while the fifth day is a traditional time for married women to visit their parents.

The eighth day is known as All Gods, and the ninth the birthday of the Jade Emperor, the ruler of Heaven. From the tenth to the fifteenth, preparations are made for the Lantern Festival (q.v.), and the parents of newborn children take lanterns to the Halls of the Ancestors in thanksgiving.

New Year's Day is everyone's birthday, and Chinese people customarily reckoned their ages, not from their birthday, but from the New Year in which they were born. It is also interesting to note that Chinese people reckon their ages cardinally, rather than ordinally; that is to say, a newborn child is in its first year, and therefore aged one. Consequently, a baby, born a week before the New Year, would be reckoned, in Chinese terms, to be aged two on New Year's day.

Nine see *Lo Shu*.

Nine Cauldrons see *Yü*.

Niu T'ou — The Ox Head Demon see *Hell; Wu-ch'ang Kuei*.

No Cha see *Li No-cha*.

No-chü-lo see *Lohan, The Eighteen*.

Nü Kua, Nü Wa This mysterious figure is the consort of Fu-hsi (q.v.), but her origins and significance are obscure. She is depicted as a beautiful woman with her lower body of a serpent. Examples have been found which also depict Fu-hsi serpent-tailed, with his own and Nü Kua's tails interwined. While the concept of Nü Kua is certainly ancient, it has not yet been established whether Nü Kua preceded Fu-hsi or followed him. What is likely is that the Creative Goddess Nü Kua was an ancient deity; that Fu-hsi was established from a different source, and that later commentators put them together as a pair. But although she is frequently said to be Fu-hsi's consort, in some accounts she is said to be his sister.

After Heaven and Earth had been separated, Nü Kua took some yellow clay, and moulded it into figures of men and women. Then tiring of the task, she took a rope, dipped it into yellow mud, and splashed the drops around. Those made from the clay became the nobility, and those from the mud drops, the poor. In later mythology she is said to be the daughter of Shui Ching-Tzu, the Water Spirit, born in 2953 BC. Her lower body was that of a snail: hence the name Nü Wa, which means Snail Maiden.

After the death of Fu-hsi, she reigned as Nü-huang. Two feudal princes, Kung Kung and K'ang Hui tried to overthrow her reign of the Element Wood by the use of the Element Water, but she countered by the use of the Element Fire. Dispelled, Kung Kung flew to the west, and seized one of the pillars which supports Heaven. This caused a hole in the heavens, and the earth to tilt. Kung Kung was, however, later captured and slain for his crimes. Nü Wa built a fairy palace in a single night, and repaired the heavens with five stones of different colours (the five elements).

She instituted marriage, and is therefore considered the patroness of marriage arrangers.

O

Ox-Boy

Old Man of the South Pole Nan Chi Hsien-weng. The very concept of the South Pole is something that must have been very difficult for the non-scientific mind to grasp, and shows the extent and influence of Chinese astronomy. Today we are so used to thinking of the world as a globe, and are familiar with pictures of the Antarctic wastes, that it is difficult to empathize with a mind that scarcely knew what lay beyond China, save that India lay to the west, the sea to the east, and cold desert to the north. Beyond that the world was unknown. The Pole Star could be seen, as could the rotation of the heavens. But where, and how, could the Chinese mind visualize the South Pole? Consequently, it was regarded as a place both elusive and mysterious. That it might possibly exist on the earth was a paradox that could only be assumed; that it was a frozen waste could not be imagined. Yet it is highly significant that Chinese mythology should be aware of the South Pole, a feature which is completely unknown in Western mythology or imaginative fiction.

The Old Man of the South Pole, the ruling deity of the Shou Hsing or Star of Longevity, was one of Chiang Tzu-ya's protecting spirits in the legendary Battle of Mu (q.v.).

He controls the deaths of mortals, and descends to Earth on the first day of the ninth month.

Om-i-t'o see *Amida*.

Oracle Bones It is just over a hundred years ago that one of the most important discoveries in Chinese history was made by chance. In 1889, a scholar was intrigued by the medicine an apothecary was preparing for his sick friend; the ingredient was called 'dragon bones'. In fact, they were ancient bones used by diviners of the Shang dynasty to record questions put to an oracle, and the oracle's response. More importantly, the bones were dated in the system of the time. It took many years to decipher the ancient script, but as more and more of the bones were found, it was found that the dates confirmed the names of kings and genealogies recorded in the classical histories of China, long thought to be mythological or invented records.

The bones used in the divination were mainly shoulder-blades, but tortoise carapaces and plastrons were also used. These were regarded as being more accurate. The bones could be used more than once. A small depression was drilled in the bone, and then a heated bar was applied. Cracks formed, and from the shape of the crack the diviner read the answer.

What is actually astonishing about the discovery of oracle bones (several tens of thousands have now been recorded and interpreted) is that Confucius had despairingly written 'What can we know about the Shang? There are no documents and no sages.' Two and a half thousand years later, his complaint was answered and refuted. (See also *Chiang Tzu-ya*.)

Ox-Boy and the Weaving Maiden Ch'ien Niu, the Ox-Boy, herdsman to the gods, fell in love with Chih Nü, the Weaving Maid, the celestial seamstress. They were, however, so taken up with each other that both cattle and loom were neglected. The gods were so displeased that the Queen of Heaven took her hairpin, and with one sweep across the sky, rent a boundary between them. Since that time the Ox-Boy, represented by the star Altair, and the Weaving Maid, the star Vega, have been separated by the River Han, known to us as the Milky Way. Happily, once a year they are able to meet, for magpies build them a temporary bridge across the river on the seventh day of the seventh moon.

What is remarkable about this legend, is that the stars representing the two characters in the tale do not now match up with the nearby constellations of the Ox and the Maiden. However, several thousand years ago, owing to the phenomenon known as the precession of the equinoxes, the relative positions of the stars and their respective constellations would have been reversed, showing that the legend must be of great antiquity, even before the invention of writing.

See also *Tung Yung*.

Ox Head Demon see *Hell; Wu-ch'ang Kuei.*

Ox, The Spring The Mang Shen is a clay figure which is taken into the fields at the spring equinox, and broken up. In all probability, it is a symbolic gesture, a vestige of what would in earlier times have been a human sacrifice to propitiate the god of the soil. There are precise instructions, in the Book of Rites, on how the Mang Shen should be prepared, with regards to its colour, size and decoration.

The first page of every Chinese almanac (q.v.) has an emblematic picture of an Ox being led by a herdsman, who may be facing towards or away from the Ox, a youth or an old man, shod or bareheaded, or with other distinctions. This token portrayal of the Mang Shen is prepared according to astronomical lore, and is deemed to reveal the nature of the coming year's harvest.

P

The Five Poisonous Creatures

Pa Ch'a (Pa Cha) God of Grasshoppers, whose worship protects against locusts and other damaging crop pests.

Pa Ch'a was a peasant of Mongolia who lived in an arid region where there were swarms of poisonous creatures, but he seemed impervious to their venom. In China he is represented with the upper part of his body human, with a beak and bird's claws and feet, and a bell for an abdomen. On the bell is written the message: 'When the kingdom is secure, the people are at peace.' In one hand he holds a gourd containing an insecticide, and an implement — hammer, sword, or even ingot — bearing the inscription, 'I catch flying pests.' The reason that he is shown with a bell for an abdomen is the result of a bizarre error which rather curiously translates almost exactly into English. An instruction to an illustrator in the distant past confused *chung*, bell, with *ch'ung*, insect, just as a carelessly written note today might substitute bell for belly.

Pagoda The pagoda is a familiar feature of the Chinese landscape. Its purpose is now mainly ornamental, and it may be built very much as eighteenth-century landscape gardeners erected follies on hillsides to add to the view. The Chinese pagoda, however, has a rather more distinguished history than that of an aesthetic amenity. It was introduced to China from India, where it had the function of being a reliquary for the bones or some revered possession of a saint. As such, it is distinctively bell-shaped and known as a *stupa*; an alternative name is *dagoba*, reliquary, from which the word *pagoda* is a corruption. Nowadays pagodas may be erected to commemorate some event or personage, or may be added to the landscape to avert bad feng-shui (q.v.). They may be circular or octagonal, occasionally hexagonal or even square, but they must have an odd number of storeys.

Pagoda Bearer see *Li Ching*.

Pa Hsien see *Eight Immortals*.

Pai-ho T'ung-tzu The White Crane Youth. A disciple of Yüan-shih (q.v.) who aided the generals of Wu Wang in their contests against the Shang. (See also Ch'iung Hsiao; *Mu, Battle of*.)

Pai Lung The White Dragon. See *Lung Wang*.

Pai-so sheng A plaited and knotted cord tied round the necks or wrists to bind the person to Buddha. See Mi-lo Fo.

P'an Chin-lien Most of the immortals, spirits and divinities who people the pages of Chinese mythology have either been mortals raised to the status of gods, or gods who have been given mortal form. In virtually every case, their lives and deeds are things of wonder. But the story of P'an Chin-lien from the novel *The Golden Lotus* is quite different. It is a very human tragedy, and the apotheosis of P'an Chin-lien was decreed neither by imperial edict, nor by celestial messenger, but by common consent.

A certain Wu Ta-lang, having recently died, left a young widow, P'an Chin-lien, in the charge of his brother, Wu Sung. She was closing an upstairs window when Hsi-men Ch'ing, a wealthy merchant, passed her house. Glancing up, he saw the widow and was immediately smitten by her beauty. He made enquiries about her, got himself introduced to her, and soon became on very intimate terms with her. So intimate were these terms, in fact, that one day Wu Sung returned to find the couple at their love-making. The merchant made his escape, but the enraged brother-in-law cut off the woman's head in one stroke.

She has now become immortalized, perhaps unkindly, as the Goddess of Brothels.

P'an Ku The legendary architect of the universe. Oddly enough, the story of how P'an Ku created the universe is now so firmly established in Chinese folklore, it would be forgivable to assume that the story of P'an Ku was one of China's earliest legends. However, the great philosopher Ssu-ma Ch'ien (q.v.) makes no mention of it, and in fact P'an Ku does not make his first appearance until the fourth century AD. The legend, ascribed to the brush of Ko Hung (Kung) (q.v.) is likely to have been a tale imported from South-East Asia. It is highly unlikely that it would have been fabricated by a Taoist writer such as Ko Hung, because it would have been second-nature to an educated Chinese writer to introduce established characters of Chinese mythology, but none are present. The date of its composition may be even later, as its first appearance may not be earlier than the eleventh-century Wai Chi (Records of Foreign Lands). The substance of the legend is that P'an Ku chiselled the universe for eighteen thousand years, and as he chiselled, so he grew himself, six feet every day. When his work was complete, his body became the substance of the universe: his head became the mountains, his breath the wind. From his eyes the sun and moon were made, while the stars were made from his beard. His limbs became the four quarters, his blood the rivers, his flesh the soil, his hairs the trees and plants, his teeth and bones the rocks and minerals, and his sweat the rain. Finally, the lice on his body became the human race.

P'an Ku is represented as a dwarf clothed in a bearskin, or in an apron of leaves, with horns on his head. He holds the hammer and chisel with which he formed the universe, and is surrounded by the Four Creatures: Tortoise, Phoenix, Dragon and Unicorn (see *Celestial Emblems*).

P'an Kuan The Registrar of Hell, usually depicted holding a book with people's names. Now used as the term for an assistant to a higher deity, the role of Registrar of Hell having been passed to Chung K'uei (q.v.).

Pan-t'o-chia see *Lohan, The Eighteen*.

Pao-chih. Buddhist monk. See *Chih Kung*.

Pao-kung Ch'an-shih [Ban Gong the Zen Scholar] see *The Vanishing Monastery*.

Pao Ssu Concubine of Emperor Yu of the Chou dynasty (781–771 BC). Although she was extremely beautiful, she never smiled, and the

Emperor was forever trying to find ways to amuse her. The country had a signalling system of beacon fires to be lit in the case of invasion. To amuse Pao Ssu, the Emperor caused the fires to be lit, so that thousands of soldiers were mustered. When she saw the panic that was caused by the alarm, the girl laughed. As it had given her so much amusement, the Emperor repeated the performance a few times more. The Emperor so doted on Pao Ssu that he dismissed the Empress, Lady Shen. Her father was so angered that he united with a foreign tribe, the Ch'üan Jung, to attack the Emperor. Inevitably, when the Emperor was genuinely under attack, the beacon signal was ignored, and the Emperor overthrown.

Paradise Although the stars and constellations were regarded as the abodes of the gods, the paradises (two of them) for earthly souls had a terrestrial location: to the west was the Western Paradise on Mount K'un Lun (q.v.), and to the east the Isles of P'eng-lai (q.v.).

Hsi T'ien, the Western Paradise, was in Han times the abode of Hsi Wang Mu (q.v.), the Queen Mother of the West, but after Buddhism had become the dominant religion of China, it became the home of Kuan Yin, a female manifestation of Buddha. Though its ruling deity may have changed, the location remained a beautiful garden situated on a mountain, with marvellous flowers, lakes and birds. But whereas the soul had to undertake a journey full of treacherous pitfalls before it could reach K'un Lun, it was only necessary to repeat the name of Buddha constantly to be admitted to the Western Paradise, either immediately, or after a period of transition. (See also *Human spirit*.)

Peach Peaches are an emblem of long life, sacred to Hsi Wang Mu (q.v.). As a consequence peachwood is the most potent medium for charms and talismans.

Pearl Believed to be a distillation of the essence of the Moon, exuded from the mouths of dragons. For this reason dragons are usually depicted with stylized balls of flame in or near their mouths.

P'eng-lai Shan The Mountain of P'eng Lai, in the Eastern Isles, the ultimate paradise of the Taoists. Possibly Sumatra, or some other South Sea island from which sailors brought tales of blissful idylls, gave rise to the legend. In Han times, expeditions were despatched to find the Isles of P'eng-lai, though presumably, those who found them never bothered to return. However, it was later revealed that the P'eng-lai Isles could not be reached by mortals, because they were surrounded by 'weak water', *ju shui*, which could support neither a boat nor a swimmer. The only means of access was therefore by air, a form of transport reserved for immortals and birds, of which there were a great number.

According to the Taoists, the P'eng-lai Isles are the home of the Eight Immortals (q.v.). The houses there are of gold and silver, the birds and animals all white, the trees of coral with pearl fruit, and all the flowers sweet-scented and in abundance. The fountains produce the water of life, and those who drink it never die, for only Immortals live there.

P'eng Tsu One of the ancients revered as the God of Long Life. He became an orphan at 3 years old, and entered the service of the Emperor Yao (2356 BC) and then Shun (2255 BC). He became a minister of state in 1324 BC, and eloped with a palace lady in 1258 BC. He outlived nineteen wives and his fifty-four sons. (See also *Fu Lu Shou*.)

P'eng Tsun see *Lo-hou and Chi-tu*.

Pheasant An ornamental bird much admired by the Chinese, it is sometimes identified with the Feng-bird or Phoenix (q.v.).

Phoenix Phoenix is used as a translation for Feng, or Feng Huang, the sacred bird of Chinese mythology. It has many miraculous attributes, but not self-rejuvenation, and does not possess the Arabian phoenix's propensity for self-immolation. It is usually portrayed as a beautiful bird, virtually identical to an ornamental pheasant. Few illustrations match its verbal description, as it is said to have the front of a swan, the hinder parts of a unicorn, the throat of a swallow, the bill of a chicken, the neck of a snake, the stripes of a dragon, and the arched back of a tortoise. Its plumage is of the five mystical colours — black, white, red, green and yellow, and it has twelve tail feathers, except in years when there is an extra month, when there are thirteen. It feeds on bamboo seeds, lives in the branches of the dryandera tree, and drinks from fountains of fresh water.

It is one of the four emblems of royalty, usually associated with the Empress. The expression Dragon and Phoenix signifies wedded bliss. In many respects its symbolism has been confused and merged with that of the Red Bird, one of the four Celestial Emblems (q.v.).

There is, however, another mythological bird, the Luan, which also has a claim to being a phoenix. It is said to resemble the phoenix at birth, but changes to a five-coloured Luan as it grows older. Its cry contains the five notes of the Chinese musical scale.

Pig (a) The last of the twelve animals (q.v.) of the Chinese zodiac.
(b) A character in the romance 'Journey to the West' (q.v.). See
Chu Pa-chiai.
(c) Seven pigs, the stars of the Great Bear, draw the chariot of Chun
T'i (q.v.). See also *I-hsing*.

Pi-hsia Yüan-chün The Turquoise Cloud Princess who presides over
childbirth. The Emperor Wen Wang (1231–1135 BC) met a young lady
weeping, and asked her the cause of her grief. She explained that her
father was the God of T'ai Mountain, and her husband the God of the
Western Sea, realms that were separated by the country of K'uan-t'an,
so perfectly governed that clouds did not pass over his land, and the
winds did not dare to blow there. As she usually travelled through the
skies, wafted by the breezes, she was unable to make her journey
home. Wen Wang therefore summoned the governor of that virtuous
land, and once he was away, the wind blew and the rains came, and
the young lady continued her journey. (See also *Yü Nü*.)

Pin-tu-lo see *Lohan, The Eighteen*.

P'o The life in a human body. See *Human spirit*.

Po I-kao Eldest son of Wen Wang (q.v.), and a victim of the wicked
T'a Chi (q.v.).
  When Chou Wang (q.v.) had imprisoned Wen Wang, Po I-kao tried
to effect his father's release by sending various kinds of tribute gifts
as ransom. These included harem girls, a magic carpet which had the
effect of making whoever sat on it immediately sober, and a highly
intelligent white-faced monkey. T'a Chi tried to seduce Po I-kao, and
being rejected, tried to bring about his downfall. Having failed to
convince Chou Wang that Po I-kao had made advances to her, she
claimed that the monkey had been sent to murder the king. This
brought the monkey's execution but not Po I-kao's. He brought his
own downfall by trying to persuade the Emperor that his relationship
with T'a Chi was unwise. For this the youth was chopped into pieces
and made into pies. These were sent to Wen Wang, with the orders
that he should eat them; his refusal would provide an excuse for his
execution. Wen Wang, however, having divined the evil purpose
through the I Ching (q.v.), ate three of the pies.
  Po I-kao was elevated by Chiang Tzu-ya (q.v.) to be ruler of the
constellation Tzu Wei (q.v.).

Poison The occupation of ancient Chinese pharmacists was not confined to the preparation of medicines and elixirs, but also included the manufacture of poisons, although the two were often confused. Cinnabar (mercuric sulphide) was, and is still, prescribed as a potent drug. One specific poison, *ku*, was considered so virulent that its manufacture was forbidden under pain of death. It was prepared by putting several venomous insects into a sealed jar and left until they had devoured each other. The survivor, having acquired the venom of its fellows, was then distilled into a toxin. Readers familiar with the I Ching (q.v.) may be interested to know that this is the original meaning of the title of Hexagram 18. This is revealed in the Chinese character, which represents three stinging insects over a dish.

The Five Poisonous Creatures of classical allusion are the toad, often shown three-legged, the scorpion, spider, snake and centipede, although there are occasional variations. Pictures of these are often used as charms, particularly on the fifth day of the fifth moon, when they may be attached to the cross-beam of a roof, or worn by children to protect them from childhood diseases.

A tincture of the Five Poisons is made by putting the five creatures into *samshu*, a liquor. The resulting horrible fluid is left in bowls outside the shops of rich merchants, for the delectation of poor persons who may be passing, not with a view to their extinction as might at first be thought, but to provide a remedy for coughs and rheumatism for those unable to afford the services of a physician.

The lizard, also considered by some to be venomous, is called the Protector of Palace Virtue. If they are fed on cinnabar, and their tails cut off, the blood, when rubbed on the wrist of a virtuous woman, will be indelible.

Po-che-lo see *Pu K'ung*.

Po-lo-t'o-she see *Lohan, The Eighteen*.

Porridge see *La Festival*.

Po-shih A Taoist priest in the time of Ch'in-shih Huang-ti (221–209 BC). The Emperor expressed a wish to see the famous Chan (q.v.), a sea-monster which could build towers from its breath. Po-shih said he would ask the God of the Sea for permission to visit. Then the Emperor asked to visit the country where the sun rose. Po-shih said could be effected quite simply, and conjured a bridge out of the sea. However, when they tried to cross, one of the courtiers offended the Sea-God, and the bridge sank beneath the waves.

Po-t'o-lo see *Lohan, The Eighteen.*

Pu K'ung (Po-che-lo) The founder of Tantric Taoism. He arrived in China from Ceylon in about AD 733, visited the court at the capital, Ch'ang-an, and proceeded from there to Lo-yang.

He brought more than 500 sutras, devised an alphabet for the transcription of Sanskrit terms, and instituted the Festival of Hungry Ghosts, Yü-lan Hui.

He wanted to retire to India in 749, but was prevented by the Emperor Hsüan Tsung, and remained at court under the reign of three generations of T'ang Emperors.

He was famed for his charms and talismans, and his ability to bring rain. This he did by erecting a platform covered with coloured cloths, and a small wooden figure which, on being supplicated, would move its eyes and teeth. Rain would then follow.

Q

Queen of Heaven

Queen Chen Ch'en-ssu, brother of Emperor Wen Ti (AD 220–7), fell in love with the Empress, Queen Chen, and dedicated love poetry to her. But the Emperor was furious, and had her shut up in a dungeon. He then changed the title of the poem to Elegy on the River Lo, dedicating the poem to the River Spirit, Mi Fei, daughter of Fu Hsi. But Queen Chen died in the dungeon, and returned to the river, where she has listened to the songs and poetry of scholars down the ages.

Queen Mother of the West see *Hsi Wang Mu.*

R

Rebus (yü)

Rabbit or Hare The fourth animal of the Chinese zodiac (q.v.). The Hare features prominently in Chinese cosmological paintings, and may be seen singly, or as a pair, pounding the drug of immortality in a large vat. The story of the Hare in the Moon is one of the lost legends of China. Although various theories have been put forward for its introduction from other countries, there is no doubt that the Hare, and its connection with the elixir of life, is an indigenous Chinese myth, and it is featured in many early Chinese paintings and artefacts, such as the Banner of Ma Wang Tui (q.v.).

The Moon Rabbit is a prominent figure at the Mid-autumn Festival (q.v.). (See also *Ch'ang O.*)

Rahu see *Lo-hou and Chi-tu.*

Rahula see *Lohan, The Eighteen.*

Rat Despite being the first animal (q.v.) of the Chinese zodiac (q.v.), there is little in Chinese mythology to suggest a reason for its prominence. This is one piece of evidence to support the theory that the twelve animals were an Indian invention.

Rebus The Chinese language abounds with homonyms (words which sound the same but have entirely different meanings, such as raze and raise). There are, for example, more than a hundred different Chinese characters with the pronunciation *chi*. This means that it is not only possible, but very simple, to make visual puns to convey hidden messages. Thus, a lettuce, *fat choy* in Cantonese, signifies good luck: also *fat choy*.

Auspicious pictures might illustrate some or all of the following.

Bat	fu	Good luck
Bottle and saddle	p'ing an	Peace and security
Chalice	chüeh	Dignity
Fish	yü	Superabundance
Horse and pearl	ma pao	Success in examinations
Lobster	ha	Laughter
Stag	lu	Promotion

Red The colour of the element Fire, and the South. It is regarded as an auspicious colour, and is usually used as the colour for a bride's wedding dress, white being associated with funerals. The Chinese have several words for red, one being the orange red of cinnabar (mercuric sulphide), and another a deeper red to indicate Imperial approval. When referring to documents written in red by the Emperor, the expression is often poetically translated as the mark of the 'vermilion pencil'.

Ren see *Jen*.

Rice Wine Dream see *Eight Immortals,* Lü Tung-Pin.

Rooster The tenth of the twelve animals (q.v.) of the Chinese zodiac (q.v.). Oddly to us, in the eastern reckoning of time the Rooster hour represents the sunset time of day.

Ruyi see *Ju-i*.

S

Shun

Sacred Books of China There are nine ancient sacred books which, with one exception (the I Ching (q.v.)) have close parallels with the books of the biblical Old Testament. The nine books are divided into Five 'Ching' classic texts composed before Confucius, and Four 'Shu', books written after Confucius. The remaining four Ching are the Shu Ching, 'Book of Documents' a terse historical record; the Shih Ching, 'Book of Poetry'; the Li Chi 'Book of Ritual'; and the Ch'un Ch'iu 'Spring and Autumn Annals', another chronicle. The compilation (but not the authorship) of the books is attributed to Confucius (q.v.) and there is no reason to doubt this, although of course the original authorship is quite unknown.

The four Shu are post-Confucian, and consist of the Lun Yü, the 'Analects' or Sayings of Confucius; the Ta Hsüeh, or 'Great Learning' by a disciple of Confucius; the Chung Yung 'Doctrine of the Mean' by the grandson of Confucius; and the Meng Tzu, the Book of Mencius (q.v.).

The oldest texts are the Shih Ching and the I Ching, and date from the Shang dynasty (1765–1122 BC) or earlier. However, many of the places and names of an even earlier dynasty, the Hsia, recorded in the documents of the Shu Ching have been validated by archaeological evidence.

Sakyamuni Shih-ch'ia-mou-ni, the name preferred by Chinese Buddhists to Gautama, the historical personage, the founder of Buddhism. Usually represented sitting cross-legged on a lotus, eyes half-closed in meditation. (See also *Buddha; Buddhism*.)

San Ch'ing The Three Pure Ones, the Taoist Trinity. They live in Three Celestial Palaces. The first of the Pure Ones, Yü Ch'ing, the Jade Purity, lives on the Jade Mountain. From him proceeds all truth. This highest throne is occupied by Yü Huang (q.v.).

The second palace, the Shang Ch'ing, or Higher Azure Palace, is occupied by the Tao Chün, who controls Time, the yang and yin, and has existed eternally. The third palace, the Highest Azure, is occupied by Lao Tzu. (See also *Yüan-shih*.)

Sha Ho-shang The Priest Sha. Character in the Journey to the West (q.v.). A former minister in the Jade Emperor's palace, he dropped and smashed a crystal bowl, and was exiled from the Heavenly Kingdom. On earth, he was born as a monster who devoured passers-by, and as a punishment was wounded every seventh day on the neck by a mysterious sword. However, Kuan Yin (q.v.), on her way to China to find an adventurer bold enough to travel to India and bring back the Buddhist scriptures, released him from his torments. He vowed to lead a virtuous life, and helped Hsüan Tsang on his journey.

He is usually portrayed with a necklace of nine skulls, trophies of former Chinese emissaries to India, who never completed the return journey. (See also *Monkey King*.)

Shaman see *Wu*.

Shang Ti Lord on High, the ancestral deity, and the nearest equivalent to the Western concept of one God. He governs, rewards and punishes. He was revered both as a vegetarian spirit who was the internal soul of the plant itself, and also as the remotest ancestor. The concept of the Supreme Being held in Confucian times, but became modified in time. He was later seen as a kind of Emperor presiding over a court of supernatural beings. His Prime Minister was Kuan Yü (alternatively Kuan Kung, or Kuan Ti (q.v.)). Under him were the city gods, beneath them the T'u Ti, the Earth God (q.v.) of the locality, and finally the Tsao Chün, or Stove God, for each family.

The term was adopted by earlier Christian missionaries as the word for God (that is, the God of Abraham) but later rejected because of the inevitable confusion.

Shang Tu see *Xanadu*.

Shan Hai Ching The Book of Mountains and Rivers. A vividly imaginative geography of unknown authorship written about the third century BC, perhaps based on earlier writings.

Sheep The eighth sign of the Chinese animal zodiac. The Chinese word *Yang* also translates as Ram or Goat, something which needs to be borne in mind by the student of Chinese astrology. Attempts to equate the Chinese zodiac with the Western one point to the fact that both zodiacs include a sheep and an ox. But the fact that the Ox of the Chinese zodiac, and Taurus of the Western zodiac are both the second signs is purely chance, and has to be set against the fact that the Sheep of the Chinese zodiac and Aries are directly opposite each other. (See also *Animals, Twelve; Five Rams of Canton; Zodiac.*)

Shen Kung-pao According to legend, a former colleague of Chang Tzu-ya (q.v.), when he was in the service of Chou Wang. He tried to persuade Chiang Tzu-ya to return, and attempted to destroy the list of future immortals. (See also *Mu, Battle of.*)

Shen Nung According to the histories, the second Emperor of China of the legendary era, and declared to have reigned from 2737 to 2697 BC. The son of Princess An-teng and a celestial dragon, his element was Fire, and so he is sometimes known as Yen Ti, the Ardent Emperor, as the character for 'ardent' consists of the character for 'fire' repeated.

He is said to have built the first plough, taught the practice of husbandry, discovered medicinal herbs, and instituted markets. He is also credited with having extended the EIght Diagrams (q.v.) as formulated by his predecessor Fu Hsi (q.v.) into the sixty-four hexagrams of the I Ching (q.v.).

Shen Wan-san Fourteenth century, born in Nanking. A fisherman sometimes worshipped as the God of Riches, owing to his finding a magic bowl, *chü-pao p'en* (q.v.). He presented this to the Emperor Hung Wu (1368–99) who used it as a bomb to blow down the city-gates of Nanking. She was posthumously titled Guardian of the Territory of the Capital. This somewhat confused legend seems to have originated through the use of the term *chü-pao p'en* for a kind of grenade which Shen Wan-san may have invented.

She Wang The Snake King. Said to be an apotheosis of Fang Cheng-hsüeh, who had a split tongue, and lived during the Ming dynasty. Having been tutor to the son of the King of Shu, he was appointed

an adviser to Emperor Hui Ti (1399–1403). When the Emperor
committed suicide, Fang Cheng-hsüeh entered the service of the new
Emperor, Ch'eng Tsu. But Fang Cheng-hsüeh was overwrought by Hui
Ti's death, and despised the new Emperor so thoroughly that when
he was asked to write out a proclamation, he threw his writing-brush
to the floor and cursed the monarch. For this he was executed.

On the day before the funeral of Fang Cheng-hsüeh's grandmother,
his father dreamt that an old man had advised him to move house,
on account of the fact that ditch-diggers were about to kill all the
snakes they found. Simultaneously, his mother, who was pregnant,
dreamt that snakes were about to reincarnate themselves in her womb.

In the legendary Battle of Mu, the Snake King was Ch'ang Hao, who
had the protean ability to transform himself into numerous shapes
before being finally vanquished.

Shih-ch'ia-mou-ni See *Buddha, Sakyamuni.*

Shih Kan Tang Stone tablets, carved with the characters Shih Kan
Tang, meaning, the Stone Dares to Resist are frequently erected
opposite bridges, roads at T-junctions, and other places where the
feng-shui (q.v.) is adverse, to deflect the malign influences that might
otherwise be channelled along a straight, man-made path.

The origin of the custom, however, dates from the times of the feudal
states (a few centuries BC) when the Shih (Stone) family adopted the
motto Kan Tang. Some feng-shui stones are additionally carved with
the name of the Eastern Mountain and other potent demonifuges such
as tiger's head motifs. Their use for feng-shui purposes is first
described in books of the eighth century AD, but the probability is
that the custom was well established by then.

Shih Tien-yen-wang The Ten Departments of Hell (q.v.).

Shou Hsing The Longevity Star, inhabited by the Old Man of the
South Pole (q.v.).

Shun Emperor of mythological times, 2317–2208 BC, renowned for
his good and humane government. He succeeded the Emperor Yao,
who favoured him in place of his own son. Shun is said to have had
double-eyes. His father married a second time, and having another son
by his second wife, took a dislike to Shun and tried several times to
kill him. Despite this, however, Shun behaved with patience and
fidelity, and heads the list of the Twenty-Four Examples of Filial Piety
(q.v.).

Shu-po-chia see *Lohan, The Eighteen.*

Smallpox, God of see *Tou Shen*.

Snake The sixth of the Twelve Animals (q.v.) of the Chinese zodiac (q.v.). In the earliest Chinese dictionary, the Shuo Wen (Speech Signs) written in AD 120, long before the animal names were in general use, the sixth branch, Ssu, is described as having the shape of a snake, and could be the reason why Buddhist scholars may have used the snake for the sixth of the twelve branches (q.v.).

While dragons are deeply engrained in Chinese legend, snakes are much less common, being introduced into later legends through the influence of Hinduism, and connections with *naga* (snake) worship. In the earliest legends, Nü Kua (q.v.) is described as having a snake's body and a woman's head, and is thus depicted in the Banner of Ma Wang Tui (q.v.). Fu Hsi (q.v.) is occasionally represented in the same manner, but not always. Decorated tiles and bricks of the later Han dynasty (*c.* first and second centuries) sometimes show Fu Hsi and Nü Kua as two human-headed snakes intertwined.

Although snake temples are no longer extant in China, there is a remarkable Taoist Snake Temple, in the Chinese quarter of Penang, Malaysia. Offerings of frogs and other serpentine delicacies were formerly offered to the Snake King at Suchou, Kiangsu. Live snakes are sometimes carried in procession in honour of She Wang (q.v.) the Snake King on the twelfth day of the fourth moon.

Sodomy, God of see *Cho Wang*.

Spring Ox see *Ox, The Spring*.

Ssu-ma Ch'ien *c.* 145–85 BC. The Grand Historian of China. It is to Ssu-ma Ch'ien that we owe much of our knowledge of ancient China's history and legend. His father was Ssu-ma Tan, the hereditary Recorder and Grand Astrologer to Wu Ti (q.v.), and Ssu-ma Ch'ien succeeded him. He began work on a complete history of China, complete with treatises on scientific subjects, and biographies of notable persons, as well as historical records.

In 98 BC, he came to the defence of a friend who had been unjustly punished by the Emperor. For his temerity, Ssu-ma Ch'ien was sentenced to death, but in order to complete his monumental work, he underwent the greater disgrace of castration. His writings not only preserved China's history up to his lifetime, but also served as the model for all other official dynastic histories compiled by the scholars of the succeeding dynasty.

Sun Hou-tzu see *Monkey King*.

Su-p'in-t'e see *Lohan, The Eighteen*.

T

Three-Legged Toad

T'a Chi Executed, 1122 BC. Reviled as the wickedest woman in Chinese history, she was the concubine of Chou Hsin (Chou Wang, q.v.) the last Emperor of the Shang dynasty, and one of the main reasons for his being so. Those who dared to oppose her were forced to walk along a greased copper pole suspended above a pit of fire. Chou Hsin was eventually defeated by Wu Wang (q.v.), and T'a Chi taken prisoner. She was, however, possessed of such a powerful personal enchantment that when the time came for her execution, no one dared to strike the fatal blow. Finally, an old counsellor, T'ai Kung, covered his face and delivered the nation from the last symbol of its tyranny. (See also *Po I-kao, T'ai Sui*.)

T'ai Sui Literally, The Great Year; The God of Astrology; also, the Ministry of Time (q.v.).

The T'ai Sui, or Counter-Jupiter, is described in Ssu-ma Ch'ien's treatise on astrology, written in the second century BC. As the planet Jupiter's speed is less than that of the Earth's, it appears to be travelling backwards, and a counter-planet was invented to track its imaginary forward movement. The cycle taking twelve years, the twelve divisions of the sky occupied by the imaginary counter-Jupiter also corresponded to the twelve monthly divisions of the solar year.

Manuscript calendars of the Sung dynasty often portray the T'ai Sui as the Minister of Time, surrounded by twelve officials representing the twelve years of the Jupiter cycle. In a manuscript dated AD 978, the officials are shown wearing head-dresses with animal emblems. (See *Chinese Astrology* p. 65.) In the Ming dynasty, however, a few centuries later, the twelve officials are depicted as being animal-headed.

When the twelve animals (the 'branches') are combined with the ten stems they form a cycle of sixty combinations, known in Chinese as the *chia-tzu*, from the first two names of the stems and branches. Taoist temples which have shrines to the T'ai Sui will inevitably have a composite shrine to the sixty chia-tzu officials. These, however, are not portrayed as being animal-headed, but have human form, dressed in the rank of a high official. The statuettes portraying the sixty officials may be carefully carved, or, in poorer temples, mere blocks of wood wrapped in red paper. They are arranged on shelves in reverse order, the first, Chia-tzu, being numbered 60, the second, I-chou 59, and so forth. The reason for this is that the numbers originally represented a person's age, so that, for example, someone whose age was 59 would know that the official presiding over his destiny would be I-chou. The petitioner would then be able to offer a prayer on a slip of paper which could then be placed at the foot of the statuette, together with an offering of incense, lamp oil or money. It might be reasonably assumed that each year the statuettes would be rearranged to correspond with the calendar, but this is not the case.

The worship of T'ai Sui at altars open to the sky was instituted by T'ai Tsu (q.v.).

The T'ai Sui, or the genius inhabiting the T'ai Sui, can be the source of natural disasters, not in the region ruled by the T'ai Sui, but in the opposite region. Accordingly, if alterations to the landscape or building work are implemented in a place presently ruled by the T'ai Sui, precautions need to be taken by the residents of the area lying in the opposite direction. The position of the T'ai Sui for any year is shown in the annual almanac (q.v.).

The legend of T'ai Sui relates that he was the son of Emperor Chou Wang (q.v.) and Queen Chiang, but because he was born in a caul, he appeared to be a mass of formless flesh. The wicked concubine T'a Chi (q.v.) told the Emperor that his queen had given birth to a monster, so the Emperor gave orders for the baby to be exposed, and the Queen to be thrown from a high tower. However, the child was rescued by Shen Chen-jen, and given to the lady Ho Hsien-ku (the only female among the Eight Immortals, q.v.) to raise, and he was named Yin, that being the dynastic name of the later Shang rulers, of whom Chou Wang was the last. When he was of an age to understand, Ho Hsien-ku told him of his true parentage, and what had befallen his mother. Yin returned to his rescuer, Shen Chen-jen, and pleaded for vengeance on the tyrant. T'ien Fei (q.v.) gave him a golden battleaxe and club. He joined the army of Wu Wang (q.v.), and after the Battle of Wu, seized the Imperial Concubine and dragged her before Wu Wang. The king agreed to let Yin execute T'a Chi, but before he could slay her with his golden battleaxe, she transformed herself into smoke and disappeared.

For his bravery and filial piety, the Jade Emperor, Yü Ti (q.v.) gave him the title T'ai Sui.

T'ai Tsu 1368–99. It is said that the reason for the T'u Ti shrine being placed on the ground, rather than in a more elevated position, is due to the Emperor T'ai Tsu. During a journey, the Emperor called at an inn, but the only available table held the usual shrine to T'u Ti, the Earth God (q.v.). He ordered the shrine to be placed on the floor, giving the reason that the Earth God would be more at home closer to his own element, and the custom has been followed ever since. It is unlikely, however, that this is the real origin of the custom.

T'ang Kung-fang Achieved immortality following a test of his worthiness by Li Pa-pai (q.v.) who gave him a copy of the Tan Ching, the Cinnabar Classic, for the recipe for immortality. T'ang prepared the potion, and became immortal on Cloud Terrace Mountain in Szechuan.

Tantra see *Pu K'ung.*

Tao [Dao] The Way. An indigenous Chinese religion and philosophy, firmly established by the time of Ssu-ma Ch'ien (q.v.). The basic tenets of Tao were gathered by the philosopher Lao Tzu (q.v.) and given further substance by Chuang Tzu. The argument of Tao was originally in opposition to that of Confucius: Confucius believed in strong central government and administration, such as existed in the time of the Chou dynasty, and looked towards the ancient emperors Yao and Shun as examples of model authority. Lao Tzu, however, favoured the simpler life of a rural economy, and praised the age of the Yellow Emperor and Shen Nung, when the Earth was at its Garden of Eden stage. Thus Confucius emphasized the importance of direction and example; Lao Tzu that of self-discipline.

In 213 BC the Ch'in emperor Shih Huang Ti, finding philosophers at variance with each other ordered the Burning of the Books (q.v.) in an attempt to make a fresh beginning for all learning. A new form of Taoism developed, one which owed much to shamanism and spirit worship, and very little to the writings of Lao Tzu. Encouraged by the court of Wu Ti, Taoists pursued the quest for magical recipes for the elixir of life and the philosopher's stone.

The coming of Buddhism saw an increase in the Taoists' activities as they competed with the visible manifestations, the temples and literature, of the new religion. The two main religions waxed and waned according to the whims of the ruling court. In 555, Wen Hsüan Ti, Emperor of the Northern Ch'i states, tried to establish some kind of order, and set the Buddhists and Taoists in debate. With the Buddhists succeeding, the Taoists were obliged to adopt the Buddhist faith.

More drastic measures were adopted by the first T'ang emperor, Kao Tsu (reigned AD 618-27), who for the first five years of his reign suppressed religious practices altogether. A century later, however, Taoism was given a new lease of existence with the founding of colleges, with examinations, under the T'ang emperor Hsüan Tsung (reigned 713-56). He also bestowed the title of Tao Teh Ching (the Canon of the Way of Virtue) on the works of Lao Tzu, the name by which the writings are still known, added his own commentary, and decreed that the book should replace the Confucian Analects as a standard text for study, although it was in turn replaced by the I Ching (q.v.) a few years later.

The pendulum swung back in favour of Buddhism in the ninth century, when another T'ang emperor (also coincidentally called Hsüan Tsung (reigned 847-60), although the Chinese characters are not the same) abolished Taoism in favour of Buddhism because the previous emperor Wu Tsung had suffered a serious injury to his throat, rendering him speechless, through drinking a putative elixir of immortality.

Since the eleventh century Buddhism and Taoism have been interdependent, often needing to join forces against the inroads of other beliefs. Kubla Khan (q.v.) in the thirteenth century attempted to restore Taoism to its fundamentals, and ordered the destruction of all Taoist books apart from the Tao Teh Ching. The Emperor K'ang Hsi (reigned 1662-1723) condemned Taoism, Buddhism and Christianity as false doctrines, but this did not prevent his support of them.

To summarize in brief, there are basically two forms of Taoism: the popular kind is concerned with the exorcizing of demons, the provision of charms and spells, potions and medicines, while the fundamentalist Taoism, following the writings of Lao Tzu and Chuang

Tzu, decrees a simple, contemplative life. In this respect, Taoism has undergone the kind of development shared by Buddhism and Christianity, as seen by the elaborate rituals played out in Tibetan lamaseries and Catholic cathedrals, when compared with the simple life followed by those who prefer to break away from the pomp and procession of the established religion, whatever it may be.

Tao cosmology All cause and effect is due to the Tao, the Way. The Way can be explained as the reason or cause of everything which followed. Before the Tao there was no existence, Wu-wu: Not Nothing, but with the Tao came Wu Chi: No Limit. From the No Limit Chaos, Hun T'un, evolved, and within this chaos there became the first fixed point in space and time, the T'ai Chi, the Great Pole. From the T'ai Chi came the T'ai I, the Great Change, which went through the first stage of T'ai Ch'u, the Great First, in which there was Hsing, or Form, and a second stage, T'ai Shih, the Great Beginning, in which there was Ch'i, or Breath. Form and Breath combining produced T'ai Su, the Great Primordial, which had Chih, or Substance.

If we substitute proportion for Hsing (Form), energy for Ch'i (Breath), and matter for Chih (Substance), we come very close to present-day concepts of the physical constitution of the universe. In the first matter, the first atomic particles, are the two charges, positive and negative, in Chinese Yin and Yang. From this point, however, Taoist cosmology differs from modern physics in saying that all things, both terrestrial and celestial, fall into one of five groups, the Wu Hsing, or Five Elements (q.v.) of Wood, Fire, Earth, Metal and Water. (See also *Hun T'un.*)

Tao-jen Literally, a Taoist person. Used of someone who practises Taoist magic, as distinct from a monk or ordained Taoist priest.

Tao Mu see *T'ien Mu.*

Tao-nü Literally, a Tao-woman, more specifically a sorceress or medium who might communicate with spirits, or provide cures and medicines; the equivalent of a 'wise woman'. (See also *Mu-jen.*)

Ta Yü Yu the Great. See *Yü.*

Tea Chinese daily social life revolves around *ch'a,* or tea. No house would fail to have tea permanently at hand, while the invention of the vacuum flask means that no one need ever be more than a few feet from water, hot enough to make an infusion of the leaves. Yet Marco

Polo never mentioned it in his journals, and the first mention of *ch'a* in Chinese literature does not appear until the sixth century. The Ch'a Ching, the Book of Tea, was written about AD 780 by Lo Yü, now revered as the patron deity of tea.

But although *ch'a* was late arriving on the scene, other brews were known to the ancients; there is a reference, *c.* 50 BC, in a book by Wang Pao to someone boiling a decoction of *t'u* which had been bought in Szechuan. Hua T'uo (d. AD 208) noted that drinking *t'u* makes people think better. At that time, however, the plant would have grown wild, as tea cultivation was not introduced until the T'ang dynasty (AD 618–907).

Three deities are revered as the patron of tea: Lo Yü, Ling Tzu (in north China) and Sung Su-k'ung.

Ten-day week The earliest written Chinese texts, on oracle bones, include signs which are used to identify the days. At that early period in history, a ten-day week was in use by the literate classes, the seven-day week not reaching China until the fifth or sixth centuries AD. The ten day-names are (1) Chia, (2) I, (3) Ping, (4) Ting, (5) Wu, (6) Chi, (7) Keng, (8) Hsin, (9) Jen, (10) Kuei. These ten names are known as the Ten Stems.

As the Chinese word for day is the same as the word for sun, there emerged a legend to the effect that at one time there were ten suns. At night the ten suns rested by the Heaven Pool, and sheltered by the Fu-sang tree, but when they climbed to the top of the tree, their great heat scorched the earth and all living things. Consequently, the Emperor Yao (q.v.) had them shot down, as a result of which all the birds fell out of the sky.

The legend is one of the oldest known in China, and antedates by centuries most of the legends of Chinese religious and popular literature, including the story of P'an Ku (q.v.), the Chinese equivalent of Adam. The Fu-sang tree, with nine of the ten suns, is shown in the banner of Ma Wang Tui (q.v.), painted in the Han dynasty around 202 BC.

An important historical point is that emperors of the Shang dynasty all bore titles that included one of the ten stems, as for example, Chou Hsin, the last of the Shang emperors. As the order of the stem names is quite random, they were obviously not used as a form of numeration. They may record the day of accession, however.

Ten Stems see *Ten-day week.*

Ten Suns see *Hou I; Hsi Wang Mu; Ten-day week.*

Ten Thousand Spirits, Battle of see *Mu, Battle of.*

Thousand Character Essay An extraordinary primer, formerly the second book to be learnt by schoolchildren. It consists of one thousand characters, all different, arranged into 250 sentences of four characters each. The amazing jigsaw was said to be the brainchild of a certain Chou Hsing-ssu, of the sixth century AD, who completed the puzzle in a single night, though the effort drained him of all his strength, and by the next morning he had turned into a white-haired old man.

Three Religions, The Confucianism, Taoism and Buddhism, represented by the three patriarchs, Confucius, Lao Tzu and Buddha, often shown together in religious pictures.

T'ieh-kuai Li Li T'ieh-kuai. God of the apothecaries. Fifth of the Eight Immortals (q.v.).

T'ien Fei see *T'ien Hou*.

T'ien Hou (Tin Hau) Niang-niang Goddess of Sailors, also known as T'ien Fei, Heaven's Concubine, while Chun T'i (q.v.), Goddess of Light, is also known as T'ien Hou. The various origins ascribed to this divinity may be due to the fact that T'ien Hou is actually an amalgamation of a number of legendary figures.

Her father's name is variously Lin Yüan, Lin Ling-su, or Ts'ai, her mother Ch'en or Wang, her birthplace Fukien or Chekiang, her dates AD 713-56, 907-60, 960-77 or 1101-26.

According to the Taoist legend, she was the daughter of fisherfolk. One day she dreamt that her parents were out in their boat, caught up in a terrible storm. She ran and pointed out to sea, and her parents' boat returned safely to shore, the sole survivor of the fleet.

The reason for the extraordinary title, Heaven's Concubine, is given by a Taoist authority as the fact that Heaven the Emperor, is male, the Earth the Empress, female, and that the T'ien Fei, the Concubine, represents the female element of Heaven.

She is worshipped by navigators, and by those wanting children. Because of her maritime connections, she is the most popular deity among the Boat People of the Southern seas, who celebrate her anniversary on the 23rd day of the Third Moon.

Pageants, processions, displays and theatricals entertain the great crowds who gather at the T'ien Hou temples, outside which various contests of skill are also held. It is customary to make offerings of cardboard clothes, paper coinage, incense and similar combustible items, while using the occasion to make an outdoor picnic. (See also *Tou Mu*.)

T'ien Kou The Celestial Dog; name of a star. In mythology, the celestial dog consumed the moon during eclipses, and had to be shot down by the Archer, Hou I. In common with most of the celestial residents, he makes a brief appearance in the story of the Monkey King.

T'ien Mu see *Tou Mu*.

Tien Ts'ui Shih Her mother-in-law being old and toothless, and unable to take solid food, the girl nursed her with the milk from her own breast. She is distinguished by being the only female among the Twenty-Four Examples of Filial Piety (q.v.).

Tiger The third animal of the Chinese zodiac (q.v.). A White Tiger is one of the Celestial Emblems (q.v.). (See also *Vampires and werewolves*.)

Time The T'ai Sui (q.v.) is the Ministry of Time, presided over by Yin Chiao, and with the following committee members:

1. Wen Liang, Day Duty
2. Chiao K'un, Night Duty
3. Han Tu-lung, Accumulation of Happiness
4. Hsieh O-hu, Bearer of Misfortunes
5. Fang Pi, Guide
6. Fang Hsiang, Herald
7. Li Ping, Year Superintendent
8. Huang Ch'eng-i, Month Superintendent
9. Chou Teng, Day Superintendent
10. Liu Hung, Hour Superintendent

The last four officials, however, were annihilated in the Battle of the Ten Thousand Spirits, which took place on the overthrow of Chou Wang (q.v.).

Ti Mu see *Wen Ch'ang*.

Ting Lan Han dynasty. One of the Twenty-Four Examples of Filial Piety (q.v.). After Ting Lan's mother died, he made a wooden figure of her which he and his wife treated as the living mother. A neighbour coming to borrow some kitchen utensil, the wife asked the figure for the proper permission by means of divining lots (Ch'im, q.v.). The reply was negative, whereupon the neighbour, furious, struck the wooden effigy. When Ting Lan returned home, the mother's expression showed displeasure, and his wife told him the cause. He then went and beat the neighbour with a stick, for which he was arrested. But when he gave his explanation, and the magistrate came to see the figure, it was seen to shed tears. This incident becoming widely known, he was given high honours. A more prosaic version of the story, however, says that when the divining lots refused to give permission, it was the wife who struck the figure, whereupon Ting Lan divorced her.

The special ruler used by practitioners of Feng-shui (q.v.) for measuring harmonious dimensions for furnishings is known as a Ting Lan ruler.

Tin Hau see *Chun Ti; T'ien Hou; Tou Mu*.

Ti Sha (Earth Curse) The collective name for seventy-two stars of evil omen.

Ti-tsang Wang The Earth-Womb King, Supreme Authority of the Underworld, superior to, and distinct from Yen-lo Wang, the King of Hell. Ti-tsang Wang is the deliverer of souls from their Earth-Prison, Ti-yü. He is worshipped on the thirtieth day of the seventh moon, and if the month only has twenty-nine days (Chinese months vary in length from year to year) there is no ceremony.

The origin of the human representation of Ti-Ts'ang Wang is extremely confused. During the reign of the Emperor Su Tsung of the T'ang dynasty (AD 756–63), a foreign Buddhist monk, Chin Ch'iao-chio, said to be from Sinlo in Korea, and of noble if not royal descent, landed at Kiangsu and proceeded to the Chiu Hua Shan, Nine Flower Mountain on the banks of the Yangtze-kiang, Anhui.

He established a cult, and had many followers. He died at 99 years of age, sitting cross-legged in his coffin. Three years later his tomb was opened and the corpse was found to be in a perfect state of preservation — a sure sign of holiness. His disciples gave him the title Chin Ti-tsang (Golden Earth Womb), and later the title of deification, Ti-tsang Wang.

Because Chin Ch'iao-chio was accompanied by a minister named Wei-t'o, which has the same sound as the name of Wei-t'o the Buddhist Guardian of Temples, the two were inevitably confused, and statues of Wei-t'o were frequently placed next to those of Ti-tsang Wang, although there is no other connection.

Ti Yü The Underworld. See *Hell*.

Toad, Three-legged A very ancient legend, known in the Chou dynasty, says that a three-legged toad lives in the Moon, and devours it during eclipses. The toad was formerly Ch'ang O, wife of Hou I, the Celestial Archer. She had stolen the elixir of life from her husband and fled to the Moon to escape his wrath. Although she attained immortality, it was in the guise of the three-legged toad. (See also *Eight Immortals*, Chang Kuo Lao; *Liu Hai; Lohan, The Eighteen*, Nakula; *Ma Wang Tui*.)

Tortoise One of the Celestial Emblems (q.v.), the symbol of longevity and wisdom. It is said that its shell represents the vault of the universe. A common symbol for longevity is the Tortoise and Snake, whose union was thought to have engendered the universe.

The reason why the tortoise symbolism has been superseded by the Black Warrior as the emblem of the North, is probably due to the fact that 'tortoise' is a term of abuse.

Tou Mu The Mother of the (constellation called the) Ladle, i.e. the seven brightest stars of the Great Bear. She is also known as T'ien Mu, Mother of Heaven, and Tao Mu, Mother of the Tao, and the seven stars of the constellation are frequently shown on banners and flags flying outside Taoist monasteries. (See also *Chun T'i*.)

Tou Shen The Spirit of Smallpox. During the reign of Chou Wang (q.v.), the last Emperor of the Shang (Yin) dynasty, Yü Hua-lung was the governor of an important fortress situated in a bend of the Yellow River (Huang Ho). Yü Hua-lung attempted to wipe out the opposing army by spreading smallpox through the enemy camp, perhaps the earliest recorded examples of germ warfare. Wu Wang (q.v.), his general Chiang, and most of his soldiers were struck down with the illness. According to legend, Chiang sent to the mythical emperor Fu Hsi (q.v.) for the antidote, which was transmitted by Shen Nung (q.v.). The generals and the army were saved, but left pock-marked. Chiang then ordered a revenge attack on the fortress. Yü Hua-lung's five sons, Ta, Chao, Kuang, Hsien and Teh, were killed in the attack, and Yü Hua-lung committed suicide.

The five sons constitute the subordinate ministers of smallpox, governing the East, West, South, North and Centre. (See also next entry.)

Tou-shen Niang-niang A Taoist goddess, usually depicted wearing a shawl to protect her from the cold, who protects against smallpox. She had four sons: Sha Shen aids recovery from scarletina; Chen Shen protects against the measly stage; Ma Shen helps to remove the disfigurement after recovery; P'an Shen averts the final fatal stage of black smallpox. (See also T'ien I-Yüan.)

Trades and Professions, Patrons of Just as there are patron saints in Western countries for various trades and enterprises, even though the existence of the saint may have been doubtful, so in China, every profession and calling must have its patron, taken from the lists of the immortals, spirits, or even works of fiction. No list would ever be complete, for even the compilation of a list would generate a patron of list-compilers. A selection follows: there are further biographical details of the patrons listed under their own entries in this guide.

Barbers	Lo-tsu Ta Hsien
Beancurd-makers	Huai Nan Tzu (Liu An)
Cakemakers	Lei Tsu
Carpenters, Masons	Lu Pan
Childbirth	K'eng San Ku-niang
Cooks	Tsao Chun
Doctors	Huang Ti
Dyers	Ko Hung
Finance	Yüan-tan
Fishermen	Fu-hsi
Fortune-tellers	Kuei Ku-tzu
Hoteliers	Kuan Ti
Incense-makers	Huang K'un
Musicians	Lei Hai-ching
Needlemakers	Liu-hai Hsien
Pharmacists	Shen Nung
Potters	Lao Tzu
Prostitution	P'an Chin-lien
Quicklime-burners	Ho Ho
Sailors	T'ien Hou
Sauce-makers	Lei Tsu
Scholars	Wen-ch'ang
Silk-weaving	Lei Tsu
Smallpox	Tou Shen
Sodomy	Chou Wang
Tailors	Huang Ti
Tea	Lo Yü
Vintners	Tu K'ang

Ts'ai Shen God of Wealth. The accolade is usually bestowed on Chao

Kung-ming of the twelfth century BC. He was formerly a hermit living on Mount Omei, then, in the wars against Wu Wang (q.v.) joined the army of Chou Wang (q.v.). Riding a black tiger, he threw pearls which burst like grenades. Chao Kung-ming was a dangerous force and seemed to be invincible, so the general of the opposing side, Chiang Tzu-ya (q.v.), resorted to witchcraft. He made a straw figure, wrote Chao's name on it, and offered incense before it for twenty days, before finally shooting peachwood arrows into the figure's eyes and heart. Simultaneously, Chao Kung-ming fainted and died. After the war was over, Chiang Tzu-ya praised Chao Kung-ming's bravery, regretting the unmanly means used to bring about his defeat, and installed him as God of Wealth.

Another Chao Kung-ming, who died in AD 229 and was the brother of Chao Tzu-lung, a famous hero, was probably the real claimant to the title, the foregoing legend having been attached to his name centuries later.

A less common claimant to the title is Yüan-t'an P'u-sa, a Muslim, usually shown riding a tiger. He holds a knotted cudgel, and has a magic bowl called the *ch'ü-pao p'en*.

Buddhists show the Ts'ai Shen as a large-paunched figure, also holding the *ch'ü-pao p'en*.

The Ts'ai Shen is generally regarded as the patron deity of merchants. Pictures of wealth-trees, symbolizing the attributes of Ts'ai Shen, show their branches made of strings of coins, and the fruits gold ingots.

Other contenders are Kuan Kung and Shen Wan-san (q.v.), and Wu-ch'ang Kuei (q.v.).

Ts'ai Shun Lived at the time of the rebel Emperor Wang Mang, *c.* AD 25. One of the Twenty-Four Examples of Filial Piety (q.v.).

During the famine caused by the revolt, he collected berries, giving his mother the ripe ones, and eating the unripe ones himself. During the period of mourning, while keeping watch over the coffin, he was told that his house was burning down. However, he remained by his mother's body's side, and when he returned home, the house was untouched. Two anecdotes illustrating his filial piety are also related of others. As his mother had been frightened of thunder, he used to visit her grave during storms to comfort her spirit, which is also said of Wang Ai (q.v.), and the telepathic rapport that he had with his mother is also ascribed to Tseng Shen (q.v.).

Tsang Fang Haunted houses. See *Ghosts*.

Ts'an Nü The Silkworm Maiden. There are four deities who are known by this title: the first person to breed silkworms (not necessarily a woman); a young lady who became a silkworm; the god of the star T'ien-ssu; and the wife of the Huang Ti, the Yellow Emperor (q.v.)

The legend of Ts'an Nü relates that in the time of King Kao Hsin-shih (2436–2366 BC) there lived a beautiful girl, Ts'an Nü, with her parents. One day her father was kidnapped by robbers. For a whole year nothing was heard of him, until eventually Ts'an Nü's mother, despairing of ever seeing her husband again, offered her daughter in marriage to whoever would bring him back. At that moment, their horse broke out of the stables and galloped off. Several days later, the father returned riding the horse. The family were overjoyed, but strangely, from that time on the horse was restless, neighed incessantly, and would not eat. They were puzzled until the mother remembered the reward she had promised. They refused to acknowledge that the promise applied to horses, and when the horse became more fractious, the husband killed it.

In accordance with the usual practice, the dead animal was skinned to make leather, and the hide hung out to cure. But when Ts'an Nü passed the hide, it suddenly twitched, encircled her, and vanished into thin air, taking Ts'an Nü with it.

Images of Ts'an Nü are worshipped on the third day of the third moon for the successful cultivation of mulberry trees and silkworms. Because of the horse's head and hide she is known as Ma-t'ou Niang, the Horse Head Lady.

Tsao Chün; Tsao Wang The Stove or Kitchen God, one of the most popular deities of China and formerly found in every household, just as the Earth God was found in every locality graced with a name. His image may be a paper pasted up over the stove every Chinese New Year, or less commonly, a little clay figure in a niche in the stove. One of the most charming and amusing customs in a family household occurs the week before the New Year. In order that the Kitchen God may visit the Gods of the Western Paradise, and report on the activities of the household, the paper Kitchen God is taken down, and ceremoniously burnt, perhaps with a little straw for his horse, some honey to sweeten his lips, and a little alcohol to let the paper burn more brightly, but also to get the spirit a little tipsy, so that he will make a favourable report of the household activities. Sometimes a priest is called in to make the proceedings more auspicious.

Despite the association of the kitchen with the female head of the household, the worship of Tsao Chün is always performed by the male head of the family, even to the exclusion of females from the ceremony altogether. Where the household has a shrine to Tsao Chün, this is carried into the courtyard, and a table laid with cakes, preserved and fresh fruits, meats and snacks. Incense is burnt and offered to the shrine, children light fireworks, and the ceremony ends with the burning of the paper portrait.

Legends concerning the origin of the Kitchen God are legion. One relates that a certain Chang Tsao-wang married a young lady called Kuo Ting-hsiang, but though she was faithful and tender, and helped him to prosper, he fell in love with another called Li Hai-T'ang, a lady whose virtue, if not easy, was not very apparent. She persuaded him to divorce his wife and marry her instead. However, without his former wife, Chang's fortunes dwindled, and Li Hai-T'ang left him. Chang fell on bad times, lost his sight and became a beggar. One day, he chanced on the house of his first wife, who took pity on him and gave him a dish of his favourite noodles. He began to cry, saying that they were as delicious as those his former wife used to make. With that, she said, 'Chang Lang, Chang Lang, open your eyes!' and he recovered his sight immediately. Realizing where he was, he was so filled with shame and remorse that he jumped into the fire and was burnt to death. Ting-hsiang tried to save him, and grasped his leg, but it came away from his burning body. Ever since then, the rake used for the ashes has been called Chang Lang's leg.

Many other suggestions have been made as to the origin of the Kitchen God, among them that he was actually Yen Ti, the Ardent Emperor (see Shen Nung) because Fire is repeated in his name, or the Yellow Emperor, Huang Ti (q.v.) because he was the first to build a stove.

As for the actual origin of the custom itself, the probability is that the Kitchen God was instituted by poor families in imitation of the ancestor worship of their richer neighbours. However, it is also said that during Han times, a Taoist alchemist, Li Shao-chün, had petitioned the Kitchen God for eternal youth, and the ability to exist without food. Li approached the Emperor Wu Ti (q.v.) asking him to authorize the worship of Tsao Chün, assuring him to do so would ensure the favours of the Kitchen God, who would not only endow him with immortality, but also prepare the magical recipes for making gold. The Emperor followed the Taoist's suggestions, and instituted the cult of the Kitchen God. However, the promised benefits were not forthcoming, and Li began to lose his credibility.

The Taoist then hit on a plan to trick the Emperor. He wrote some messages on silk, and gave them to an ox to eat. Li then informed the Emperor that he would find the recipe for the elixir of life in the stomach of the ox. The Emperor had the ox slaughtered, and the wonderful text was found as promised. But the Emperor was not convinced, and comparing the script with Li's own handwriting, saw through the swindle, and ordered Li's execution. By then, however, it was too late to stall the worship of the deity, and the popularity of the practice increased, continuing to the present day.

The foregoing account is, of course, apocryphal. The first historical reference to the worship of the Stove God is found in a poem written during the reign of the Kao Tsung Emperor (1127–62), which touches on the custom outlined above, the inference being that the custom was by then widespread and well known.

Apart from the New Year ceremonies, the official day of worship for Tsao Chün is the third day of the eighth moon, and for his wife the twenty-fourth of the same month.

Tsao Kuo-chiu The Fourth of the Eight Immortals (q.v.).

Tsao Wang Chang Tsao-wang, the Kitchen God. See *Tsao Chün*.

Tseng Shen 506–450 BC. One of the chief disciples of Confucius, and considered to be the author of part of The Great Learning, one of the Confucian Classics. Whenever he was away from home, and his mother wanted him to return, she would bite her finger, which the son felt sympathetically. One of the Twenty-Four Examples of Filial Piety (q.v.).

Tsui-erh Heroine of one of the folk-tales of Lu Pan (q.v.). Tsui-erh was in love with Li Ching; though they were due to marry, her widowed mother could not afford to buy her a wedding dress. One day, a passing traveller asked if he could lodge with them while he found work, and the two women took pity on him. As a stone bridge was being built across the river nearby, the old man offered his services to the master mason. The master thought that the stranger would be too old and feeble to be of much use, but nevertheless he agreed to let him help in dressing some of the stone blocks. However, much to the irritation of the master mason, and to the scorn of the other workers, the stranger seemed to spend all his time chipping away at one particular stone which had been broken and discarded. Eventually, considering the old man to be a harmless eccentric, the master mason told the old man to leave, but agreed to let him keep the stone he had been working on in lieu of wages.

Taking the stone back to the widow's house, the old man gave it to Tsui-erh and her mother as a present, and when they asked, somewhat understandably, what possible use it could be to them, he said that they could use it for a trough. To their further bewilderment, he cautioned them that should anyone want the 'trough' they must pay for the daughter's wedding dress.

Eventually, the time came when the bridge was to be ceremoniously opened, and a great procession of officials and dignitaries, accompanied by banners and music, made its way to the riverbank. Tsui-erh and her mother went to join the crowd of sightseers, but it became obvious that something was wrong. Everywhere there was confusion; the procession was approaching, but the bridge was still not ready. The keystone for the arch did not fit. Without it the bridge would collapse under the weight of the procession, and there was no time to dress a new stone. It dawned on Tsui-erh and her mother that their 'trough' was the same size as the missing stone, and they hurried home to fetch it. Just as they thought, and to the astonishment of the master mason, the 'trough' that the old man had been working on fitted exactly, and the master mason was more than happy to pay the price the old woman asked — a wedding dress for her daughter. As the keystone was lowered into place, it dawned on the master mason that the strange old man must have been none other than the grand master mason himself, Lu Pan.

Tsun-che A title following a person's name, meaning Venerable.

Tu Fu AD 712–70. Celebrated Chinese poet. The Eight Immortals of the Wine Cup feature in his poetry. The circumstance of his death are ironic. Close to starvation having been isolated by a flood for ten days, he then died through over-eating.

Tu K'ang Together with I Ti (q.v.), revered as the discoverer of wine. He belonged to the later Chou dynasty, roughly the sixth century BC. He died on a day marked by the tenth branch (q.v.), which in old Chinese characters represents a wine-bottle. Vintners and distillers therefore close down on a tenth-branch day. At the temple of Shun, in Chi-nan, Shantung, there is a stream called Tu K'ang which is reputedly where Tu K'ang first made wine.

Tung-fang Shuo A famous magician of the Han dynasty at the court of Wu Ti (q.v.), patron of silversmiths and goldsmiths; the spirit of the Year Planet (Jupiter), also of the Metal Planet (Venus).

His family name was Chang, his personal name Shao-p'ing. The 'Accounts of Spirits and Deities' gives his biography in great detail. Tung-fang means Eastern, and Shuo First, the explanation being that he was born on the first day of the month. Three days after he was born his mother died, and the child was exposed. An old lady found him and as there was light in the dawn sky, she called him Tung-fang.

As the child grew, it proved to be highly gifted with both intellectual and supernatural powers. Later, his skills were recognized and he was taken on at court, and even sat at the Emperor's table. One day, jars of wine, supposed to endow the drinker with immortality were presented to the Emperor. Tung-fang Shuo, invited to taste it, enjoyed it so much that he drank most of it, leaving hardly any for the Emperor. When the Emperor, enraged, ordered his execution Tung-fang Shuo replied that if the potion worked, execution would have no effect, and if it didn't, the potion would have been a fraud.

In 103 BC he presented the Emperor with ten trees, each nine feet high, which gave off musical sounds, which he had brought back from a visit to Hsi-na-hsieh. If the wood of the trees sweated, it foretold illness, if they broke, death. In 93 BC one of the trees which the Emperor had returned to Tung-fang Shuo broke. The magician called his three sons to his death bed; a dragon appeared, and carried him on its back to the sky. Shortly after that, the star Sui-hsing, which had not been seen for sixty-nine years, reappeared in the sky. Since there was no body, the Emperor buried Tung-fang Shuo's clothes on Chung-ch'iu Mountain, P'ing-yüan.

Tung Yung The name given to the Ox-Boy (q.v.) in the following legend, said to have taken place in the reign of the Emperor Ching Ti (156–140 BC).

Tung Yung's father having died, the son despaired because he could not afford to pay for a decent funeral. Consequently, he went to a certain Fei of An-lu, and bound himself in service for a substantial loan. Shortly after doing this, he met a beautiful girl who asked him to marry her. When he agreed with alacrity, she took him back to the creditor and asked what the man wanted to release her husband from his bond. Fei demanded three hundred bolts of cloth. The girl set to work, and within a month, she had completed the task and paid off the debt. Then she explained to the grateful but astonished husband that she was really Chih Nü (q.v.) the Weaving Maiden of the gods, who had sent her to reward Tung Yung for his act of devotion to his father's memory. Thereupon she left the mortal world, but miraculously sent him two sons within the year.

The tale of Tung Yung is cited as one of the Twenty-Four Examples of Filial Piety (q.v.), usually illustrated in Chinese almanacs.

Tu-o Chen-jen A magician at the court of Hsi Wang Mu (q.v.). He lived in the Eight Clouds Sparkling Cavern, and was tutor to Li Ching (q.v.). He gave Heng and Ha (q.v.) their miraculous weapons, and is named in a number of later stories.

T'u-ti see *Earth God.*

Twelve Branches see *Animals, Twelve.*

Twenty-Four Examples of Filial Piety Filial piety is a clumsy term, but universally used, to convey the meaning of *hsiao*, regarded by the Chinese as one of the cardinal virtues. It is not restricted to son and parent relationship, but also includes the responsibilities of a government to its people. The legendary Emperor Shun, for example, was said to have kept harmony in the country through the exercise of *hsiao*. His devotion to his parents, who detested him, earned him the first place in the traditional list of the twenty-four models for humanity. Remarks on each of the Twenty-Four Examples of Filial Piety will be found under their own headings.

1. Shun, 2317–2208 BC
2. Wen Ti, d. 157 BC
3. Tseng Shen, 506–450 BC
4. Min Sun, 551–479 BC
5. Chung Yu, 543–480 BC
6. Lao Lai Tzu, Chou dynasty
7. Yen Tzu, Chou dynasty
8. Yung Yung, AD 200
9. Chiang Keh, AD 499
10. Huang Hsiang
11. Wang Yang, AD 265
12. Wu Meng, *c.* AD 312
13. Kuo Ch'ü, 2nd century
14. Yang Hsiang, Han dynasty
15. Ts'ai Shun, *c.* AD 25
16. Lu Su, 1st century
17. Wang Ai, 3rd century
18. Meng Tsung, 3rd century
19. Yu Ch'ien-lo, AD 500
20. Tien Ts'ui Shih
21. Chiang Shih, Han dynasty
22. Ting Lan, Han dynasty
23. Chu Shou-ch'ang, Sung dynasty
24. Huang T'ing Chien, 1045–1105

Tzu A term added to names with various meanings. Literally, it means child, but added to the name of a person of nobility, it signifies Prince, as in Huai Nan Tzu. By extension, it signifies a wise man or philosopher, as in Lao Tzu, Chuang Tzu and others.

Tzu Wei The Purple Crepe Myrtle; name of the god who inhabits the North Polar Star. In Chinese astrology, the Purple Palace is the name given to the circumpolar region of the Heavens, that is, the stars which are near the Pole Star, and therefore visible throughout the year in the northern hemisphere. Because the Pole Star represents the Emperor, the stars of the Purple Palace are regarded as being of prime significance. Tzu and Wei (written in different Chinese characters but having the same sound as the characters for Purple Crepe Myrtle) are also the names of two Chinese algebraic signs which are significant in the first steps of drawing up a Chinese horoscope. It is more than likely that this combination of characters generated the concept of the Tzu Wei deity. (See also *Po I-kao.*)

U

Unicorn

Unicorn The Chinese unicorn, the Ch'i-lin, could discern the guilty from the innocent. It aided Kao-yao, Judge to the Emperor Shun, by spiking the guilty with its horn. It has been conjectured that the belief is a folk memory from some ancient method of trial by ordeal. The Ch'i-lin has the body of a deer, the tail of an ox, the hooves of a horse, and a single horn, which is described as fleshy. It has hair of different colours on its back, and yellow hair underneath. It is herbivorous, and has the power to walk on grass without crushing it. It was believed that a light made by burning the Ch'i-lin's horn conferred the ability to see into the future by staring into a bowl of water.

The appearance of the Ch'i-lin was an indication of the reign of a good and just Emperor. In 1414 a giraffe was sent as tribute to the court of Yung Lo, the third Ming Emperor, and as it had many points of resemblance to that of the Ch'i-lin, it was said by the flattering courtiers to be an auspicious omen.

Unpredictable Ghost More accurately, the Ghost of Impermanence. See *Wu-ch'ang Kuei*.

V

Vampire

Vampires and werewolves Belief in vampires is not confined to the people of Transylvania. If the *p'o*, or human spirit (q.v.) is not released at death, the corpse (q.v.) may be animated, as the following anecdote illustrates.

Li Chiu, a pedlar of Huo Shan, finding no lodging, was obliged to spend the night in a temple. During his sleep, Wei-t'o (q.v.), the Protector of Temples, appeared to him in a dream, warned him of impending danger, and told him to hide behind his statue. Li Chiu woke up in time to see a coffin open and a vampire emerge. Following the advice given in his dream, he jumped behind the statue of Wei-t'o just as the vampire sank its fangs into it.

Half-humans who were able to transform themselves into marauding beasts are no strangers to Chinese folklore. The most frequently encountered metamorphosis is that of the fox spirit (q.v.), but in Shansi, where wolves were formerly a menace, there are several tales of people who roamed at night in the guise of a wolf. The mother of Wang Han of T'ai Yuan was such a creature. She had a voracious appetite for raw meat, and would go abroad at night in her animal shape, until she was spotted by one of the maids. However, when she overheard the family discussing the problem, she made her escape and was never heard of again. Fortunately, the mother had not acquired a taste for human flesh, unlike that of a young odd-job man in the same province, active in AD 765, whose lycanthropic activities included the devouring of plump little children. Somewhat unwisely, he boasted of his successes to the father of one of the children he had consumed. In a rage, the father struck him with an axe, and the dying beast changed into a wolf.

Were-tigers have been a constant cause of dread, not just because of the threat to life, but also because the soul of anyone eaten by a tiger must entice another victim to the tiger's lair before it can be released, thus perpetuating the menace. (See also *Ghosts*.)

The Vanishing Monastery Pao-kung Ch'an-shih, or Pao-kung the Zen (q.v.) master, on his way to the White Deer Mountain, became lost, and was in need of shelter. Luckily, he heard a bell being rung, so he followed the sound until he came to the Monastery of Spiritual Retirement. It was, however, guarded by ferocious dogs, and he was about to turn back when he saw an Indian monk calling the dogs off, and beckoning him to follow him into the monastery.

To his surprise, when he got there he found that the great hall of the monastery was merely a dormitory, and the doors to the other rooms were bolted. However, he eventually came across a smaller cell with a bed, and as no one else seemed to be about, he decided to stay there.

After a while, he heard voices of the monks arriving, but could not imagine where they were coming from. Then he saw that they were entering the hall through a hole in the ceiling, from which they floated to the ground. The monks were apparently strangers to each other, for they all asked each other's names, and where they had each travelled from. It became evident that they had arrived from all parts of China, and India too.

They had just about settled when a latecomer arrived, giving the excuse that he had been detained in theological discussion with the teacher Chien-ch'an (Mirror of Zen). At this, Pao-kung explained that his own teacher was Chien-ch'an, too. No sooner had he spoken than the monks all stood up, bowed, and together with the monastery, vanished into thin air. Pao-kung found himself at the foot of a tree. He proceeded on his journey, and met Shang-t'ung Fa-shih, Shang-t'ung the Buddhist Teacher. Having heard Pao-kung's story, the Fa-shih explained that the vanishing monastery had existed since the time of Shih Chao (AD 273–332), and that it was apt to appear, disappear, and reappear somewhere else. The tolling bell was often heard by people in the vicinity, though neither the monastery nor the monks were visible to everyone.

Veda see *Wai-t'o*.

Voodoo see *Mu-jen*.

W

White Crane

Wang Ai Wei dynasty, third century. One of the Twenty-Four Examples of Filial Piety (q.v.); like Ts'ai Shun, he visited his mother's grave during thunderstorms to comfort her spirit. He could not read a certain verse in the Book of Odes, which refers to the death of parents, without breaking into tears.

Wang Chung-kao see *Huai Nan Tzu*.

Wang Mang 33 BC – AD 23. A nephew of the Han Empress Yüan Ti, who swiftly rose to high office and was appointed regent while the heir was an infant. He declared himself Emperor in AD 8 and had the infant shut off from all communication so as to be deprived of language. His reign was subsequently declared illegal, and many of those who accepted office under him have been denigrated over the centuries since.

Wang Pao see *Lo-hou and Chi-tu*.

Wang Tan (Tzu-Ming) AD 957–1017. Minister to the Sung Emperor,

Chen Tsung. His father, believing a prediction that Wang Tan and his two brothers would rise to high office, planted three locust-trees (*huai*) in front of his house to signify their destiny. As a result, the family became known as the San-huai (Three Locust-trees), the first recorded use of clan names in China.

As it happened, of the three brothers, only Wang Tan attained any lasting distinction, being raised to the nobility, made a minister of state, and on his death, canonized.

Wang Tan has a curious place in the history of Chinese mythology. The Emperor Chen Tsung was going through a period of declining popularity, and as a ruse, claimed to have had a visitation from a celestial being, Yü Huang (q.v.). The Emperor, however, knew that Wang Tan would refuse to countenance the deception, but he badly needed the support of his minister for the deception to succeed. Wang Tan was not the kind of corrupt official who could be bribed by ordinary means. So, in order to buy Wang Tan's complicity, the Emperor invited him to a banquet, and asked him whether he enjoyed the wine. When Wang Tan replied that he did, the Emperor gave him a cask of the wine to take to his family. Arriving home, Wang Tan found the cask full, not of wine, but precious pearls. He did not dare now to return the gift. Wang Tan dutifully kept silent, and so connived at the invention and creation of the supreme deity in the Taoist pantheon. In later life, however, ashamed of his feebleness, he shaved his head and became a Buddhist.

In later years, the Ch'ing Emperor K'ang Hsi (1662–1723), when asked his opinion about the incident, said that Heaven could not be accused of fraud. By inference, this meant that Yü Huang was indeed the supreme deity, and had thus engineered his own creation. Wang Tan's faults were being a flatterer during his life, and an apostate on his death.

Wang Yang AD 265. His stepmother wanting some fish, although all the rivers were frozen, he lay on the ice to melt it, so enabling him to catch a pair of carp. One of the Twenty-Four Examples of Filial Piety (q.v.).

Water see *Elements, The Five*.

Weaving Maiden see *Ox-Boy and the Weaving Maiden; Tung Yung*.

Wei-t'o (Veda) A Hindu Deva, or god, invoked by Tibetan and other Buddhists to protect monasteries. Sometimes seen at crossroads. Wei-to is represented in armour, often with a sword across his folded arms.

In temples, his statue faces inwards. He is often found in Buddhist temples guarding Kuan Yin. He is also found in Taoist temples dedicated to Ti-tsang Wang, King of the Earth's Womb, owing to a confusion of the name of Wei-t'o, Veda, with that of a certain minister (written differently in Chinese) who accompanied the historic Ti-tsang Wang (q.v.) into exile. (See also *Vampires and werewolves*.)

Wen Ch'ang, Wen Ti Wen Ch'ang Ti Ch'ün, the God of Literature; patron of stationers; holy day, third day of second moon, and also a specially selected day in the eighth moon.

There are several accounts of the life and legends of Wen Ch'ang, and they should be considered as accounts of different personalities who have been amalgamated into one. None of them are acceptable versions, because the Literary Star K'uei, and the stars forming the group Wen Ch'ang Kung, the Palace of Literary Genius, were mentioned in the astronomical treatise of Ssu-ma Ch'ien (q.v.), writing in the second century BC. All the following accounts, including the 'historical' version, apply to events which happened a thousand or so years later.

For the official historical account, Wen Ch'ang was Chang Ya, born in the kingdom of Yüeh, present-day Chekiang, but living for most of his life in Tzu-t'ung in Szechuan (Ssu-ch'uan) during the T'ang dynasty (618–906). He held a high post in the Board of Rites, but disappeared without explanation. He was canonized and received many other posthumous titles. Subsequent accounts become increasingly fabulous.

His original name was Chang Ya-tzu; killed in a fight during the time of the Chin dynasty (AD 265–316), he became Tzu-t'ung Ti-chün, the Spirit of Tzu-t'ung.

He is also credited with having fought in a battle at Ch'eng Tu in Szechuan, in AD 1000. There he thwarted a revolt by Wang Chün. Arrows with messages attached had been fired over the rebel town asking the people to surrender, but to no avail. Then a man appeared, calling to the rebels and informing them that he had been sent by the spirit of Tzu-t'ung to tell them that the town would fall on the twentieth day of the ninth moon, and not one would escape death. All happened as the stranger foretold, and in gratitude the general ordered the temple of Tzu-t'ung to be repaired.

The title Wen Ch'ang was bestowed on Tzu-t'ung in 1314 by the Emperor Jen Tsung of the Yüan (Mongol) dynasty.

Now it is necessary to introduce another element into the confused legend. The foregoing biographies can be left to one side for a moment, and we turn instead to the poor scholar, Chung K'uei. He had passed the Imperial Examinations with honours, and was due to receive the official reward from the Emperor. Chung K'uei, however, was so ugly that the Emperor refused to admit him. In despair Chung K'uei threw himself into the sea. However, an Ao, or sea-dragon, bore him on its back up to heaven. There he was invested with the responsibility and judgement of literature. He was given the constellation K'uei for his residence, no doubt because the constellation's name had the same sound as his own, even though the written character is different.

In fact, the Grand Astrologer Ssu-ma Ch'ien (q.v.) says that the Literary Star is the apex of the head of Orion, the Palace of Literary Genius consisting of six stars forming a rectangle close to it. In the past few centuries, however, the literary stars have been identified as the four very bright stars forming the rectangle of the Great Bear. Because of the astronomical connections, the image of Wen Ti is placed in a tower, called the K'uei Hsing Lou (Tower of the Star called K'uei).

Images of Wen Ch'ang are usually accompanied by four attendants: a servant, Hsüan T'ung-tzu, the Dark youth, popularly called T'ien Lung, Heaven-Deaf, and a groom, Ti Mu, Earth Mother, or Ti Ya, Earth-dumb, who looks after Wen Ch'ang's white horse.

In front of Wen Ch'ang is the attendant K'uei Hsing. Since the character K'uei comprises the characters for an imp, and the ladle (the Ladle being the Chinese term for the seven major stars of the Great Bear) K'uei Hsing is shown as a small demon holding a measuring ladle. He awards successes in examinations. The fourth attendant is Chu I (q.v.), the Crimson Gown.

Wen-chung T'ai-shih A minister of Chou Wang who fought in the historical Battle of Mu (q.v.), later apotheosized as Lei Tsu (q.v.), the Ancestor of Thunder.

Wen Ti Died 157 BC. Son of Kao Tzu, founder of the Han dynasty, and succeeded 179 BC. During his mother's sickness, he neither left her room nor changed his clothes for three years. One of the Twenty-Four Examples of Filial Piety (q.v.).

Wen Wang 1231–1135 BC; known during his lifetime as Hsi Peh, the Chief of the West, and posthumously given the title Wen Wang, the Literary King. The founder of the Chou dynasty.

He was the hereditary prince of the State of Ch'i, modern Shensi. He succeeded to the throne of Ch'i on his father's death in 1169 BC, but in 1144 BC he was denounced to the tyrant king Chou Wang as a potentially dangerous enemy. Chou Wang had him thrown into prison at Yü Li, where he spent two years in a dank and smelly cellar. To while away his time, Hsi Peh studied what fragments were then available of the I Ching (q.v.) or Book of Changes, and is traditionally regarded as being responsible for the diagrams being arranged in the sequence in which they are known today. Modern archaeological discoveries, however, do not support this belief.

Hsi Peh was at last ransomed by his son Po I-kao (q.v.), who sent Chou Wang a beautiful concubine, horses, and exotic gifts. Finally convinced that Hsi Peh was no further danger, Chou Wang set his prisoner free, and commissioned him to put down rebellious western barbarians. However, Hsi Peh was completely revolted by Chou Wang's excesses (on one occasion having been forced to eat his own son in a pie) and was reluctant to return to court. Shortly before he was about to wage war against the barbarians of the west, he decided to go hunting, and, following the custom of the time, consulted oracle bones (q.v.). The reply from the oracle was that he would not catch tigers, leopards, dragons nor bears, but a king's counsellor. Later, during the hunt, he encountered an old man fishing by the River Wei, and was so impressed by his conversation that he took him on as his adviser. The sage was Chiang Tzu-ya (q.v.), who became his counsellor, and later stayed in the service of Hsi Peh's son, Fa, who was later known as Wu Wang (q.v.). Thus, although Fa (Wu Wang, the Military King) was the first ruler of the new Chou dynasty, it was his father, Hsi Peh (Wen Wang) who is regarded as its founder.

White Of the five emblematic colours, White represents the element metal; in this case the colour is meant to be the shiny white of polished metal. In other respects, white is the colour of the occult, being the colour of those who have passed to the next world. It is unlucky to have notices of congratulation written on white paper, which would be thought as macabre as printing a wedding invitation on black-edged paper. Red is the lucky colour, so traditional Chinese wedding dresses are red for that very reason, while white is worn at funerals. The expression 'people in white garments' is a euphemism for the dead.

For that reason, albino animals are often considered to be vehicles of the supernatural, as in White Tiger (q.v.), White Crane (q.v.), White Horse (q.v.), and the White Deer in the story of the Monkey King (episode 25) (q.v.).

White Crane The White Crane is an attribute of Hsi Wang Mu, and the aerial transport of immortals and others on their journeys between this world and the next. Figures of the crane are therefore placed on coffins ready to take the soul of the departed to the Western Paradise.

Cranes are considered to be the rulers of mortal feathered birds, second only to the fabulous Feng-bird (phoenix). It is said to be extremely long-lived, and at 600 years stops taking food. It is therefore a symbol of longevity, and is usually shown near an evergreen or pine-tree, another symbol of long life.

I Kung, the Prince of Wei (c. BC 676) was so attached to a pet crane that he took it with him into battle, much to the bemusement of his forces, who gave up as a consequence and lost the battle. In AD 605, crane feathers were in great demand for ornament on the uniforms of the royal guards, and they were pursued almost to extinction. One wise bird, fearing for the safety of its young, nested high up in a tree and plucked its own feathers out so that it would survive to rear its chicks.

White Crane Youth see *Pai-ho T'ung-tzu.*

White Horse The White Horse which gave its name to several Buddhist temples features in the Journey to the West. Hsüan Tsang (q.v.) had been presented with a white horse by the Emperor to help him on his pilgrimage. He had reached Serpent Hill, where there was a deep river, when a water-monster suddenly emerged and swallowed up the horse. It so happened that the Dragon King's third son was awaiting death for a crime, and had pleaded with Kuan Yin (q.v.) to intercede for him. She agreed, and asked the Jade Emperor to release the Dragon King's son on condition that he change himself into a horse identical to the one which Hsüan Tsang originally had. He carried the monk safely to his destination and back, and the first Buddhist temple to be built was given the name of White Horse Temple, Pai-ma Miao. (See also *Monkey King.*)

White Tiger see *Celestial Emblems.*

Willow Pattern The story of the Willow Pattern Plate is a charming tale, but hardly part of authentic Chinese mythology. Nevertheless, it is now such a familiar picture that it would be an omission not to include the traditional explanation of the design. The pattern was compiled, but not copied, from Chinese sources, by Thomas Minton for Thomas Turner's porcelain factory at Caughley in 1780. Many variants of Minton's design were made elsewhere. The story was invented later as a clever marketing ploy.

The two-storey house to the right of the pattern belonged to a rich mandarin, recently widowed and retired. He had temporarily taken on a young private secretary, and as the mandarin had a beautiful daughter, they both fell in love. Knowing that the mandarin would be violently disapproving of the relationship, they had to meet in secret, but eventually the clandestine meetings were discovered. The mandarin, who had another suitor in mind for her, had a large wall built round the house to keep his daughter securely away from her lover. The suitor was rich, and presented the daughter with a box of jewels. However, while the mandarin was entertaining the suitor, the daughter and her lover met, and made off with the jewels over the bridge, hotly pursued by the father who was alerted at the last moment. They eluded him, however, and made their way to a humbler cottage until the time was safe to make their escape by boat. Sadly, they were finally apprehended; the suitor accused the daughter's lover of having stolen his jewels, and had him executed, while the girl, dreading marriage to so foul a husband, committed suicide. But in death they were united by being transformed into two cranes which forever soar above the lake.

Witches and witchcraft see *Hu; Mu-jen; Wu*.

Wong Tai Sin Huang Ta Hsien [Huang Daxian], Huang the Great Immortal. He lived in the fourth century, and is now regarded as a Taoist immortal, or saint. At 8 years of age, Huang Ch'u-p'ing (Wong Cho-ping) as he was then called, became a shepherd in Chekiang province. When he was 15, a spirit took him to a cave in the Golden Flower (Chin-hua) Mountains where he became a hermit. Forty years later, he was discovered by his brother, who had found him by following the predictions of a Taoist priest. The hermit was surrounded by blocks of white stone which, on a word, turned into the flock which had been lost forty years earlier.

Ch'u-p'ing believed himself to be an incarnation of Ch'ih Sung-tze (q.v.). The elder brother Ch'u-ch'i also became a hermit, adopting the name of Lu Pan (q.v.).

Wong Tai Sin is famous as the most popular temple for residents and visitors alike in Hong Kong. There is a hospital practising traditional medicine attached, and often, herbal remedies are chosen through the throwing of *ch'im*, or sticks, before the image of the saint. But apart from the hospital, its herb garden and medical facilities, the temple is famous for its avenue of fortune-tellers, the rent they pay providing much of the temple's income.

Branches of the Wong Tai Sin temple are now to be found in Chinese communities throughout the world.

Wood see *Elements, the Five*.

Wu (1) The transliteration *Wu* is used to represent several widely
different Chinese words. While this guide is not meant to be a
dictionary, an explanation may be useful to avoid confusion. The
commonest use of the word is the number five, and occurs in the
expressions Wu Hsing for the Five Elements, and Wu Ti for the Five
Emperors. Wu also means 'military' and was used as a title by several
emperors, as Wu Wang (Wu the King), or (Han) Wu Ti (the Han
Emperor Wu). A third meaning of the word is wizard or witch (see next
entry), while in many names, such as Wu-ch'ang Kuei, it is a prefix
indicating a negative.

Wu (2) The word may be translated as shaman, witch or wizard. They
are professional exorcists, who may also play the part of a medium
in seances to contact the dead. Their performance is rarely as
restrained as that of the European salon medium, however, being
much more violently theatrical, often accompanied by wild dancing.
In ancient times, and indeed in rural provinces of China even now,
the Wu was employed as a rain-dancer, or medicine man. In this
respect their function is not different to that of the shaman or witch-
doctor.

Chinese has several words, transliterations from Sanskrit terms,
which are easily confused with shaman. Ssu-ma Ch'ien (q.v.) writes
that Shih Huang Ti searched out *hsien-men*, which might be a
corruption of shaman. However, the Chinese word for monk, *sha-men*,
has nothing to do with Wu, being a transliteration of the Sanskrit
shramana, an ascetic.

Wu are mentioned on oracle bones (q.v.), (China's earliest written
records) and references in the classics indicate that Wu were employed
at state ceremonials, as they were in Tibet until the expulsion of the
Dalai Lama. In China, however, they gradually fell out of favour. By
the Han dynasty, although the court frequently resorted to employing
Wu for their specialist knowledge or powers, particularly in the search
for the elixir of life, they did not have the same official status that the
astrologers did. Indeed, the instance of the intervention of Hsi Men
Pao (q.v.) shows that Wu were sometimes completely out of favour with
the ruling authorities.

By the second century, female Wu were very numerous, and
gradually took on the role of leaders of the congregation in dealing
with ancestral rites and funeral ceremonies. The advent of Buddhism,
and the rival Taoism, however, gradually eroded the status of the Wu,
as these services were provided by adepts attached to the established
religions. (See also *Hu; Mu-jen*.)

Wu-ch'ang Kuei The Ghosts of Impermanence; usually translated as 'The Unpredictable Ghosts'; Messengers from Yen Wang, King of Hell (q.v.). There are two messengers, Yang Wu-ch'ang (Male Impermanence), painted white, who comes to collect the souls of those dying before their 50th year is out, and Yin Wu-ch'ang (Female Impermanence), painted black, who collects those over 50. They are accompanied by the Horse Face demon, Ma Mien (q.v.), and the Ox Head demon, Niu T'ou, being escorted to the neighbourhood by the local earth-god, then to the household by the family's kitchen-god.

Generally, when Wu-ch'ang Kuei is spoken of, it is a reference to Yang Wu-ch'ang. As such, Wu-ch'ang Kuei is usually shown with a pointed white hat bearing the four characters 'One Glance Great Fortune'. In the north of China he is portrayed with a red protruding tongue, signifying that he is the ghost of someone who has hanged himself. In southern China, he is the ghost of a man who spent three years in retreat mourning the death of his parents. When he returned home, he was in such a pitiful state that his wife refused to let him in the house and he died of grief. His office as messenger of Hell seems to have been obscured in some parts of China, where Wu-ch'ang Kuei is accepted as one of the gods of wealth on account of the inscription on his hat.

Wu Meng *c.* AD 312. He learned the magical arts from the Taoist Ting I. Among the many demonstrations of his powers was his ability to sail into the wind by waving a fan. With the help of his brothers he killed a dragon-serpent which was devastating Kiangsi. He attained immortality, as did his daughter, on instruction from the daughter of his own teacher. He is renowned as one of the Twenty-Four Examples of Filial Piety (q.v.) for keeping mosquitoes from attacking his parents, by refusing to brush them away from his own body.

Wu Shan, Fairy of The scenery of Wu Shan is among China's most spectacular. It is famed for its lofty twin peaks, and the constantly shifting cloud formations. It is reported that a prince visiting the mountains fell asleep, and dreamt that he was visited by a beautiful girl. She spread a mat for him, and placed a pillow for his head, and sang him a love-song in which she declared that she was the Fairy Princess of Wu Shan; at dawn she summoned the morning clouds, at night the rain. From this episode, the expression 'clouds and rain' has come to mean sexual intercourse.

Wu Ti (Five Emperors) The Five Emperors of Heaven. Worship of the Five Emperors, one for each of the five elements (q.v.), was Wu Ti

instituted by Shih Huang-ti of the Ch'in dynasty, the first emperor of
a unified China. He declared that until that time, there had been four
Celestial Emperors, and that he was to be the fifth. The Spring and
Autumn Annals (c. AD 239) relate:

> The birth of a new dynasty is foretold by certain signs. The reign
> of Huang Ti, the Yellow Emperor, was marked by the appearance
> of giant worms and ants, showing that the element Earth was
> dominant. For this reason, Earth was chosen as the emblem of
> the dynasty, and Yellow for the colour of the livery. Then, during
> the reign of Yü the Great (the Hsia dynasty), the auspicious signs
> were trees which did not shed their leaves in the Autumn or
> Winter. This revealed the element Wood to be dominant, and
> Green was chosen as the colour of the livery. King T'ang's
> dynasty (the Shang) was heralded by a bronze sword emerging
> from the water; so the dominant element was Metal, and the
> livery White. When King Wen (the Chou dynasty) came to power,
> there was Fire in the Heavens, and Red Birds assembled at the
> dynastic altar, thus the Fire element was dominant, and Red the
> colour of the livery.
>
> Therefore, a dynasty whose element is Water is yet to come; its
> livery will be Black, and Heaven will manifest the time by signs
> and portents. And likewise, the Dynasty of Water will come to
> an end, and a new dynasty of Earth will ascend, but that time
> is not known to men.

Taking this passage from the scriptures as his authority, Shih Huang
Ti ordered that sacrifices were to be made at the Five Cardinal Points
to each of the Sovereigns of Heaven, and had a temple to the Five
Emperors built.

Worship of the Five Emperors was suspended during the reign of
the Emperor Ch'eng Ti (32–6 BC) but restored without further
interruption on the accession of his successor, Ai Ti.

Wu Ti (Han Wu Ti) (140)–87 BC, the 'Military' Emperor, family
name Liu, reigned fifty-four years. A ruler of power and imagination,
responsible for shaping early China. His achievements were the
expansion of the canal systems, nationalization of the iron and salt
industries, the patronage of Confucian philosophy and the compiling
of the first history of China; but he also had its author, Ssu-ma Ch'ien
(q.v.), castrated for daring to criticize him.

Although he is known as the 'Military' emperor, Wu Ti gathered a
coterie of intellectuals at his court, but they inevitably included a
number of charlatans.

About 130 BC, a fang-shih (q.v.), Li Shao-chün, told Wu Ti that in order to prolong life, it was necessary first to sacrifice to Tsao Chün, the Stove God, in order to procure the vital chemical reagents needed to transmute base metal, via cinnabar, into gold. Then, drinking and eating only from golden utensils, it would be possible to prepare oneself for a visit to the Immortals on the Isles of P'eng-lai (q.v.), after which immortality would be within reach. According to Li Shao-chün, the guiding spirit was called An Ch'i, but though the Emperor followed the rituals, An Ch'i did not appear.

Wu Ti's nephew was the Prince of Huai Nan (q.v.).

Wu Ti (Liang Wu Ti) Reigned AD 483–94. The founder of the Liang dynasty. A devout patron of Buddhism. See *Chih Kung*.

Wu Wang BC 1169–1116. Family name Ch'ang, given name Fa; son of Wen Wang (q.v.), founder of the Chou Dynasty. He reputedly completed the text of the I Ching (q.v.) begun by his father Wen Wang (q.v.) during his imprisonment by the dissolute Chou Wang (q.v.).

Wu Wang led an army against Chou Wang, crossing the Huang Ho (the Yellow River) at Meng, and in a decisive action which marked the end of the Shang dynasty, routed the tyrant in the Battle of Mu (q.v.). A thousand years later, the Grand Historian, Ssu-ma Ch'ien, wrote that the defeated Chou Hsin fled to his palace, and on the Lu T'ai terrace, built a funeral pyre and threw himself into it. Remarkably, this ancient episode was verified, more than three thousand years later, by the discovery of an inscription on a commemorative bronze bowl found in 1976, which corroborated Ssu-ma Ch'ien's account even to the extent of giving the actual day of the battle: the *chia-tzu* day (first in the sixty-day cycle of the Chinese calendar) of the second lunar month (March), in the year 1123 BC.

X

Marco Polo, visitor to Xanadu

Xanadu The usual European form of Shang Tu, the Upper Capital, immortalized in Coleridge's poem. Situated some 180 miles north of Peking [Beijing] it was the summer capital of Kubla (K'u-pi-lai) Khan (q.v.), founder of the Yüan or Mongol dynasty.

According to legend, Kubla Khan built a palace with gardens of every kind of delight in abundance. Soldiers were drugged, taken to the 'pleasure dome', and when they awoke, told that they were in paradise. They were again drugged, and put on the battlefield. So anxious were they to return to the pleasures of paradise that they were eager to die in battle. Kubla Khan is said to have entertained his guests by demonstrating the loyalty of his followers; ordered to jump off cliffs to their deaths they gladly did so.

[Xian] Hsi-an. See *Ch'ang-an*.

Y

Yü

Yama see *Hell*.

Yang The active, positive, principle, as opposed to the reactive, negative, principle, Yin; in effect very close to the positive and negative qualities of atomic particles, electric currents, magnetic polarity, and the like. There is no Yang without Yin, and vice versa; all nature strives to achieve a balance of Yang and Yin. The Sun, Heaven, and Circle, male and odd numbers, are considered Yang, and the Moon, the Earth, the Square, female and even numbers Yin. Strangely, reference is always made to Yin and Yang, rather than Yang and Yin, not for any precedence given to Yin, but merely for the sake of euphony. In the I Ching, the unbroken lines are considered Yang, the broken ones Yin.

Yang Hsiang Han dynasty. When 14 years old, seeing his father about to be attacked by a tiger, he threw himself in front of it, and was devoured instead. One of the Twenty-Four Examples of Filial Piety (q.v.).

Yang Wu-ch'ang see *Wu-ch'ang Kuei*.

Yao Reigned 2357–2255 BC. The first ruler recorded in the Shu Ching, the Book of History and the model of virtuous governorship. Judging from the way that archaeological discoveries have authenticated the ancient classics, there is no reason to doubt the following very sparse biographical details taken from the Book of History. His name was Chi Fang-hsün, son of a ruler Ti Ku, and he succeeded his father as the ruler of T'ao, and then moved to T'ang. From these two places he took the title T'ao-T'ang Shih.

After ruling for many years (variously 70 or 98) he set aside his son Tan Chu and abdicated in favour of Shun, his son-in-law twice over, since he married two of Yao's daughters.

Of course, these salient facts are supplemented by fabulous tales and legends from other sources. From an ancient text, 'Edicts of the Emperor Yao', it can be presumed that he authorized the institution of some kind of astronomical observatory (see *Hsi-ho*), while the vast drainage and canal building undertaken at some distant time in the past under the supervision of K'un (q.v.) and Yü (q.v.) is also attributed to his reign.

Yellow The colour yellow is of special significance. Before the expansion of the Chinese empire had amalgamated several different states, the Chinese nation as in effect the state which occupied the area in the bend of the Yellow River. This was the centre of China, to which all the other states adhered. Thus, China was (and is still called) the Middle Kingdom, and the colour yellow, being associated with the Middle Kingdom, symbolically represents China. In addition, the word *Huang*, written with a different character, also means 'Imperial' so that Huang Ti (as spoken) may mean Yellow Emperor, or Sovereign Ruler. For this reason, yellow was also the imperial colour. The last emperor of China, Pu Yi, wrote that when a boy, he believed everything to be yellow, since he saw so much of the colour.

Yen Lo see *Hell*.

Yen Wang The King of Hell (q.v.).

Yen Tzu Chou dynasty. When his aged parents expressed a wish for deer's milk, he dressed himself in a deer's skin, and mingled with a herd until he was accepted, and so able to obtain the elusive refreshment. One of the Twenty-Four Examples of Filial Piety (q.v.).

Yi Jing see *I Ching*.

Yin and Yang Negative and positive principles; see *Yang*.

Yin-chieh-t'o see *Lohan, The Eighteen*.

Yin Chiao Son of Chou Wang (q.v.) of the Shang (Yin) dynasty. He fought against Wu Wang (q.v.) in the decisive Battle of Mu (q.v.), and was caught by Jan-teng between two mountains. Only his head was exposed, so General Wu Chi cut it off with a spade. As Jan-teng is a Buddhist figure, said to be contemporary with Li Ching, one of the Eight Immortals (q.v.), the story is probably a garbled version of the execution of Yin Chiao, who would otherwise have succeeded Chou Wang.

For another completely different version of Yin's part in the Battle of Mu, see *T'ai Sui*.

Yin Wu-ch'ang see *Wu-ch'ang Kuei*.

Yin and Yang Negative and positive principles; see *Yang*.

Yü; Ta Yü; Yu the Great Reigned 2205–2197 BC. Yü the Great; founder of the Hsia dynasty, long believed to have been a mythical era. However, archaeological evidence is beginning to reveal that classical references to names in the Hsia dynasty are not invention, but are actually based on fact. Yü is supposedly a descendant of Huang Ti, but is recorded as having been the son of K'un (q.v.) and Hsiu-chi. The records also add, however, that Hsiu-chi gave birth to him after seeing a meteor and then swallowing a pearl. His father having failed to drain the floodwaters, Yü was appointed to the task in 2286 BC, and after nine years achieved some notable success. In 2287 BC he announced the completion of his commission, as well as a survey of the country, which he divided into nine provinces. In 2224 BC, the Emperor Shun raised him to the position of Regent. On the death of Shun in 2208 BC, he began a three-year period of mourning, and ascended the throne in 2205 BC. Eight years later he made a royal tour of his kingdom, and held a Grand Assembly at Hui Ch'i (Chekiang), and had a certain chieftain, Fang Feng Shih, executed for being late. His most spectacular achievement was cutting the channel known as Yü's Tunnel (even to Ssu-ma Ch'ien (q.v.), writing in the second century BC) through the Wu Shan (q.v.) range of mountains in Szechuan. It is one of the wonders of Chinese landscape, with three successive cuttings stretching for two hundred miles.

In legend, Yü is often associated with Fu-hsi (q.v.). While excavating the channel to drain the floods, he is said to have met Fu-hsi. The sage (who like Nü-kua had a human face and serpent body) is said to have given Yü a jade instrument for measuring heaven and earth, which again infers that astronomical records were begun during his reign.

It is sometimes said that the Lo Shu (q.v.) was given to Yü rather than Fu-hsi, but the confusion is probably due to Yü's division of China into nine provinces, expressed tangibly by the Nine Cauldrons. Each cauldron, which Yü cast personally, was decorated with emblems symbolizing the province which it represented. As the power of the Hsia dynasty waned, the weight of the cauldrons dwindled. The cauldrons have been the symbols of authority, and the discovery of ritual cauldrons from previous dynasties was always regarded as an auspicious sign. The First Emperor, Ch'in Shih Huang Ti (q.v.), attempted to retrieve a cauldron from the Ssu River, but every time the cauldron was hauled up a dragon bit through the ropes.

Yüan Shih The Yüan Ching is the first principle in the San Ch'ing (q.v.), or Taoist Triad. Yüan-shih T'ien-tsun is the personification of the first principle, and is therefore the highest deity in the Taoist pantheon. But such an assertion is disputed with as much argument as surrounded the nature of the Trinity in Christian theology. Some academics argued that the Yüan-shih was not part of the triad, but above it, while others aver that the triad is superior to Yüan-shih, the highest place being accorded to Yü Huang, the Jade Emperor (q.v.).

His palace is on the Jade Mountain, Yü Shan, and its entrance is the Chin Men, or Golden Door. The Kitchen God, Tsao Chün (q.v.) reports to him on the deeds of every family on earth; his decrees are carried out by his agent Lei Tsu (q.v.), the Ancestor of Thunder.

Time past, Yüan-shih T'ien-wang would sit on a rock and preach to the crowds. When he was asked who he was, and where he came from, he merely pointed to the heavens. Eventually, a spirit, Hsüan Hsüan Shang Jen, revealed the circumstances of his miraculous birth.

When P'an Ku (q.v.) had finished chiselling the universe, his spirit had no mortal vehicle to carry it. The spirit called to Earth, and found there a virtuous hermaphrodite hermit, 40 years old, and still a virgin, subsisting on clouds and air. Each day the hermit would climb the mountains to take nourishment from the Sun and Moon. The spirit of P'an Ku was enraptured by the purity and beauty of the hermaphrodite, and waited until the mortal was about to take a breath, then entered the body as a ray of light. The hermaphrodite carried the spirit for twelve years, then gave birth through the spine. From its first moment the child could walk and talk, and took the name Yüan-shih T'ien-wang. (See also *Mu, Battle of*.)

Yüan-tan (Hsüan Tan) One of the Gods of Wealth. See *Ts'ai Shen*.

Yü Ch'ien-lo *c.* AD 500. One of the Twenty-Four Examples of Filial Piety (q.v.), who earned a reputation for his devotion to his sick father.

Yü Hua-lung see *Tou Shen*.

Yü Huang The Jade Emperor, equated with Shang Ti, the Lord of Heaven, and chief of the gods.

Despite the apparent antiquity of the myths which surround the Jade Emperor, Yü Huang was the invention of the Emperor Chen Tsung (AD 998–1023), who claimed to have had a visitation from Heaven in order to put a seal on his own authority. The Sung dynasty emperors Chen Tsung, and later Hui Tsung (1101–26), were responsible for the elevation of Yü Huang to the position of the highest deity. Chen Tsung erected a statue of Yü Huang in 1023, and made it the principal object of worship at court. Exactly a century later Hui Tsung built a magnificent temple to Yü Huang, and ordered further temples to be built throughout the empire. He then conferred the deity with the title Shang Ti, thus in effect, creating the concept of a Supreme Deity.

Although a Taoist deity, Yü Huang, under the synonymous title Yü Ti, is the Chinese Buddhist name for Indra.

The legend of Yü Huang goes as follows. There was once a king, Ching Teh, and his queen, Pao Yüeh, who had no son. They asked for the priests to pray for them, and the following night the queen dreamt that Lao Chün came riding towards her through the sky, carrying a boy child. When she woke, the queen discovered that she was pregnant. The child was handsome and wise, and succeeded his father to the throne, but relinquished it in order to follow a life of meditation. He attained perfection, and spent the rest of his days curing the sick.

Yü-lan Hui From the Sanskrit *Ullambana*; Festival of Hungry Ghosts, instituted by Pu K'ung (q.v.). One of the most colourful festivals of the Chinese calendar. On the fifteenth of the seventh moon, all the gates of Hell are opened, and ghosts are allowed to return to earth for thirty days. Offerings of rice, fruit, paper 'Hell' money, and incense are made at home to the shades of departed relatives, while similar presents are put outside for the spirits of those with no relatives on earth. Reed boats containing tiny lamps are set afloat, and elsewhere tiny oil-lamps are in profusion to guide the spirits home.

Yü-min Kuo see *Fabulous Races*.

Yün Chung-tzu A hermit who lived in the Jade Pillar Cave on Chung-nan Mountain. He appears as a marshal in the legendary Battle of Mu (q.v.).

Yü Nü The Jade Maidens, five beautiful spirits who attend Hsi Wang Mu (q.v.), one for each point of the compass (including the Centre) and dressed in the appropriate colours. (See *Elements, The Five.*) Yü Nü is also a name given to particular spirits of immortals, including Pi-hsia Yüan-chün, the Princess who presides at childbirth.

Yü Ti The Jade Emperor. Synonymous with Yü Huang (q.v.).

Z

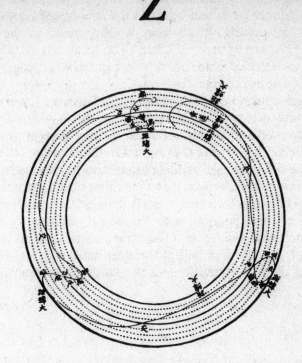

Zodiac: Mercury's path

Zen The Japanese form of the Chinese term *ch'an* (q.v.), more correctly *ch'an-na*, the contemplative or meditative school of Buddhism.

Zodiac The *zo* of zodiac means animal, and in Western astronomy and astrology the word zodiac refers to the twelve major constellations which lie along the ecliptic (the apparent path of the Sun through the sky) since most of the ecliptic constellations (but not all) have animal names. There are three features in the Chinese system of astronomy-astrology each of which may be considered to be an equivalent to one aspect of the Western zodiac.

Firstly, the well-known animal cycle, which in literal terms is more correctly identified as the Chinese zodiac, since that is what zodiac means. But the twelve animals which form the Chinese zodiac have quite a different function to the Western one. They are not the names of constellations, or any other celestial feature, but symbols used to represent a repeated sequence of numbers, 1 to 12. They are used principally to count calendar years, the hours of the day, and to a lesser extent, the days and months as well. More details are given under *Animals, Twelve*.

In the sense that zodiac means the ecliptic, for several thousand years the Chinese have used a belt of the twenty-eight constellations to identify the position of a planet or other object in the sky. (For further details, see *Mansions, lunar.*) The total belt of twenty-eight mansions is divided into 365¼ degrees, representing the Sun's progress of one degree per day.

In Western astronomy, the actual constellations of the zodiac no longer identify celestial longitude, but instead, an imaginary circle is divided into twelve equal portions each of thirty degrees, these twelve divisions being named after the original zodiacal constellations. Since the Chinese calendar uses variable lunar months, for a more accurate measurement of time, especially for astronomical purposes, the true solar year is divided into twelve exact divisions, the midpoint of the first division corresponding with the winter solstice. These twelve divisions are each divided into two, fore and aft. The aft half of one solar month and the fore half of the next make a virtual correspondence with the twelve divisions of the Western theoretical zodiac.

Table of Dynasties

Mythical rulers
  Fu Hsi (T'ai Hao)
  Shen Nung (Yen Ti)

The Five Emperors
  Huang Ti
  Shao Hao
  Chuan Hsü
  Ti K'u
  Ti Chih

The Patriarchs
  Yao   2357 BC
  Shun   2255

The Hsia dynasty   2205–1766
  Yü   2205–2197

The Shang dynasty   1766–1121
  Chou Wang   1154–1121

The Chou dynasty   1121–255
  Wu Wang   1122–1115

The Ch'in dynasty   255–206
  Ch'in Shih Huang Ti   221–206

The Western Han dynasty   206 BC – AD 25   **BC**
  Wang Mang the Usurper   AD 9–23   **AD**

The Eastern Han dynasty   25–221

The Three Kingdoms   221–65

The Chin dynasty   265–420

The Sung dynasty   420–79

The Six Dynasties   470–581

The Sui dynasty   581–618

The T'ang dynasty   618–906

The Five dynasties   907–60

The Northern Sung dynasty   960–1126

The Southern Sung dynasty   1127–1279

The Yuan (Mongol) dynasty   1260–1368

The Ming dynasty   1368–1644

The Ch'ing dynasty   1644–1911

Further Reading

Birch, Cyril, *Chinese Myths and Fantasies*, OUP, London, 1962.

Bloomfield, Frena, *The Book of Chinese Beliefs*, Arrow, 1983.

Burkhardt, V. R., *Chinese Creeds and Customs*, South China Morning Post, Hong Kong, 1982.

Christie, Anthony, *Chinese Mythology*, Paul Hamlyn, London, 1968.

Couling, Samuel, *Encyclopaedia Sinica*, Kelly & Walsh, Shanghai, 1917.

DeWoskin, K, J., *Doctors, Diviners, and Magicians of Ancient China*, Columbia University Press, NY, 1983.

Doré, Henry, trans. Kennelly, M., *Researches into Chinese Superstitions*, T'usewei, Shanghai, 1918.

Eberhard, W., *Folktales of China*, Routledge & Kegan Paul, London, 1965.

Goodall, John A., *Heaven and Earth*, Shambhala, Boulder, 1979.

Latsch, Marie-Luise, *Chinese Traditional Festivals*, New World Press, Beijing, 1984.

Loewe, Michael, *Ways to Paradise*, George Allen & Unwin, 1979.

Mayers, Wm Frederick, *A Chinese Reader's Manual*, American Presbyterian Mission Press, Shanghai, 1874.

Mong, Lee Siow, *Spectrum of Chinese Culture*, Pelanduk, Malaysia, 1986.

O'Brien, Joanne, *Chinese Myths and Legends*, Arrow, 1990.

Qi Xing, *Folk Customs at Traditional Chinese Festivities*, Foreign Languages Press, Beijing, 1988.

Walters, Derek, *Chinese Astrology*, Aquarian, 1987.

Wei Tang, *Legends and Tales from History*, China Reconstructs, Beijing, 1984.

Werner, Edward T. C., *Ancient Tales and Folklore of China*, Bracken, 1922.

Williams, C. A. S., *Outlines of Chinese Symbolism and Art Motives*, Dover, New York.